Historical and scientific sketches of Michigan : comprising a series of discourses delivered before the Historical Society of Michigan, and other interesting papers relative to the territory.

Historical Society of Michigan (1828-1861)

HISTORICAL

AND

SCIENTIFIC SKETCHES OF MICHIGAN.

COMPRISING A SERIES OF DISCOURSES DELIVERED BEFORE THE
HISTORICAL SOCIETY OF MICHIGAN, AND OTHER INTERESTING
PIECES RELATIVE TO THE TERRITORY.

Detroit:
STEPHEN WELLS AND GEORGE L. WHITNEY.
1831

Entered according to the Act of Congress of the United States of America, in the year of our Lord one thousand eight hundred and thirty-four, by STEPHEN WELLS and GEORGE L. WHITNEY, in the Clerk's office of the District of Michigan.

GEO. L. WHITNEY, PRINTER.

PREFACE.

The Historical Society of Michigan was instituted in 1829, and four annual discourses have been delivered under its auspices, bringing together the scattered facts connected with the first settlement of the country, and its subsequent history, down to the close of the war of 1812, with occasional sketches of events of a later occurrence. These discourses do not form an unbroken chain of history. Collectively, they are of a desultory character, and yet they constitute the best body of information on the subject of Michigan which is before the public. The editions of the two first discourses have been nearly, or are quite, exhausted, and the diminution of those of the two last has been in proportion to the time they have been in print.

This evidence of interest, on the part of the community, in the topics embraced by the discourses, has suggested the expediency of collecting them into one volume, and republishing them in that form, with some additional matter, properly coming within the scope of the work. The extracts from Mr. Schoolcraft's address to the Lyceum of Detroit, contain some new and interesting views of the natural history of the Territory. They are cursory, the character of the address not admitting any thing more elaborate or in detail, but they are the result of the most recent observations of a mind that has now been, for many years, habitually engaged in the subject. The remarks of Mr. Lyon on the experiment made in *boring* at Detroit are worthy of record. They give us a deep insight beneath the earth, where we had before been restricted to the surface. The facts disclosed by them, taken in connexion with the well known position of the limestone quarries at Monguagon, lying near the surface, and running across the mouth of the Detroit river, suggest new reflections as to the formation of the stony basin which is filled by the alluvion on which Detroit and its vicinity are spread. The article copied from Silliman's Journal, on the subject of the supposed tides and periodical variations of the surface of the Lakes, relates to a theory which has occupied much attention and excited no little speculation. Embracing most of the recorded data connected with it, and which alone can guide opinions to any satisfactory conclusions, the article seems to find a suitable place in this collection.

It is to be regretted that these discourses have now been suspended for two years. A perseverance, up to this time, in the plan so successfully pursued for four years, would have led to something like a fulfilment of the original design of the society. The series is now obviously incomplete. The legislative and judicial history of the Territory has scarcely been touched upon, and the long administration of Gov. Cass remains nearly unnoticed. The former will be as curious as it will be interesting and instructive, presenting to view the operation of a junction, so anomalous in our country, of the legislative and judicial powers in one body or in the same men. The framers of the ordinance of '87, aware of the anti-republican and irreconcilable association they were about to establish, no doubt intended to apply a corrective of its injurious tendencies, by making the legislative an *adoptive*, instead of inceptive, or originating power. This restriction was found in practice, as might have been anticipated, merely nominal, as the rule of modification, to suit the circumstances of the case, could have no other limit than the discretion of those who were to apply it. And the errors of legislation could, of course, find no correction in the process of adjudication, as the legislator and the judge were the same.

The history of Gov. Cass' administration will be the history of the Territory from that state of utter feebleness and desolation which marked its initial period, to the vigor and prosperity of its termination, when the Governor was transferred to a higher station.

It is hoped that these two interesting and fruitful subjects will still be brought out under the auspices of the society, whose labors may yet long be productive of useful results. Even when all the important incidents of the past, whether in obsolete print, in MS. or in tradition, shall have been gathered up, and fixed on permanent record; each passing year will still doubtless offer something in political and statistical changes, in the developement of science or the arts, which will be worthy attention and preservation.

DISCOURSE

DELIVERED BEFORE THE HISTORICAL SOCIETY OF MICHIGAN,

BY LEWIS CASS.

Introductory Remarks—Observations upon the early condition of the North American Indians—Early European Adventurers—The Sacred Fire—The Neutral Nation—Establishment of Trading Posts by the French—French Expedition to the sources of the Mississippi—Establishment of a French Post at Detroit—Description of Detroit and its vicinity—Expedition of the Ottogamies against the French and their allies—Final subjugation of the Ottogamies—Possession of Detroit and the Upper Posts by the British—Notice of the celebrated Indian Chief, Pontiac—Pontiac's design to attack the British Posts simultaneously—Destruction of Fort Michilimackinac—Attack upon Detroit by Pontiac—Interesting interview between Major Gladwin and Pontiac, at the Fort—Attack upon the Garrison—Capture of Major Campbell—Pontiac in council with the French—Attempt by the Indians to destroy the English vessels—Battle at Bloody Bridge—Cessation of Indian Hostilities—General Bradstreet arrives at Detroit—Establishment of Peace—Assassination of Pontiac—Amicable relation established between the British and the Indians—Revolutionary War between the British and the United Colonies—Expedition under Captain Byrd—Successful Expedition of General Clark against the British and Indians—Termination of the War.

DISCOURSE.

Gentlemen of the Historical Society:

The association we have formed and whose first anniversary duties have brought us together, has been instituted for the collection and preservation of such materials, both traditionary and authentic, as may enable us to trace the history of this portion of the United States, and to mark the changes it has undergone. By judicious exertions, we may hope to rescue from oblivion many important documents, to disclose many facts and transactions, either wholly unknown or imperfectly remembered, and to elucidate much that is confused and contradictory in the earlier annals of these regions. The field of labor is sufficiently interesting and extensive for all our industry and zeal.— And however rich or ripe the harvest may be, no laborers have preceded us in the vineyard.

I need not dwell upon the utility of associations formed for these objects. In our own country and elsewhere experience has demonstrated the importance of their labors.— Individuals, however ardently devoted to such pursuits, can accomplish little by solitary efforts. Unity of action, a generous spirit of emulation, the co-operation of the community, and above all a central point of union, where plans may be proposed and adopted, opinions discussed, and collections and recollections embodied and preserved, are secured by these institutions. Still less need I labor to establish the value of such memorials. In the progress of human life the present is only felt: the past is recollected, and the future anticipated. While we recall the one that we may foretell the other, the mind is withdrawn from those objects of sense which, however they may supply us with the foundations of knowledge, too often mislead us in its application. The great branches of the human family present various traits of character, various modes of life, and great diversity of changes and incidents in the history and progress of their condition, whether stationary, advancing or receding. The history of man must ever be interesting to man; and although where the arts and sciences are cultivated and flourish, this inquiry is most useful and satisfactory; still in the rudest condition of society, where nature has done much and cultivation little, there is yet abundant room for observation and contemplation.

There are no proud recollections associated with the earlier history of this region of forests and lakes and prairies. No monuments have survived the lapse of ages, to attest at once the existence of heroic achievements and a nation's gratitude. No names of renown have come down to us rescued from oblivion by their virtues or their vices.—No place is found in all our borders where the traveller can meditate upon the instability of human power, amid the evidence of its existence and decay, nor where the memory of brilliant exploits can be recalled among the scenes of their occurrence. Our country is yet fresh and green. Centuries must roll on before our arches are broken, our columns dilapidated, our monuments destroyed—before the hand of time shall have impressed upon our high deeds and high places that sanctity which enables the inhabitants of the Eternal City, even in this day of Roman degeneracy, to look back with pride to the deeds and days of the Republic. Our only monuments are the primitive people around us.—Broken and fallen as they are, they yet survive in ruins, connecting the present with the past, and exciting emotions like those which are felt in the contemplation of other testimonials of human instability.

The early European adventurers found these regions in the possession of numerous tribes of savages, divided into separate communities and speaking various languages, but having a general resemblance in their physical relations, their manners and customs, their religion, government and institutions. Much labor and research have been devoted to an inquiry into their origin and migrations. Many idle notions have prevailed respecting these topics, unworthy now of serious examination, except as they furnish evidence of the waywardness of the human intellect. That they are branches of the great Tartar stock is generally believed at the present day. Many points of resemblance, both physical and moral, leave little doubt upon the subject. But why, or when, or where the separation occurred, or by what route, or in what manner, they were conducted from the plains of Asia to those of America, it were vain to inquire, and impossible to tell.

Almost three centuries have elapsed, since Jacques Cartier, the first European adventurer, who ascended the St. Lawrence, that great artery of these regions, landed upon the Island of Montreal, then called Hochelega. He found it in the possession of a branch of the Wyandot stock of Indians, who had not long before subdued the more ancient inhabitants, and established themselves in their place. The slight notices which the historian of this expedition has left, of the appearance and situation of the primitive people who occupied this continent before us, and whose descendants still occupy it with us, leave little room to doubt, that in all the essential features of character and condition, this branch of the human family has been as stationary as any whose records are known to us. That the coming of the white man among them has on the whole been injurious, there is too much reason to believe. But those day dreams of Arcadian innocence and peace, which assigned to the Indian every moral and physical blessing till he was reft of them by the Christian spoiler, exist only where weak heads and warm hearts survey the picture drawn by their own imaginations. The present is not the occasion to examine this question. It is only necessary in confirmation of the general position, to state that the various tribes were in a state of active warfare, and of a warfare too, which was without cause in its origin, without mercy in its progress, and with no other termination, than the destruction of one of the parties.

Cartier was the pioneer, but Champlain was the founder of the French power upon this continent. For twenty years succeeding the commencement of the seventeenth century he was zealously employed in planting and rearing upon the Banks of the St. Lawrence that infant colony, which was destined to extend its branches to these shores, and finally to contest with its great rival, the sovereignty of North America. Champlain displayed, in his adventurous life, traits of heroism, self-devotion and perseverance, which, under more favorable circumstances, would have placed him in the rank of those, whose deeds are the landmarks of history.

I shall not attempt to trace the progress of these remote settlements, nor to mark the alternations of prosperity and adversity. They are peculiarly interesting to us only as they exhibit the gradual and successive steps, by which a knowledge of these internal seas, and of the countries around them, was acquired, and the settlements formed and extended. As the tide of French power flows towards this peninsula, we become more anxious to trace its principles and progress, and to inquire into the motives and means of the hardy adventurers, who were every year ascending, still farther and farther, the boundless waters before them. It was early discovered that a profitable traffic in furs could be carried on with the Indians, and the excitement of gain prompted those engaged in it, to explore every avenue, by which the camps and hunting grounds of the Indians could be approached. A better and nobler feeling, too, brought to this work, a body of learned and pious men, who left behind them their own world, with all its pleasures and attachments, and sought, in the depths of remote and unknown regions, objects for the exercise of their zeal and piety.—The whole history of human character furnishes no more illustrious examples of self-devotion, than are to be found in the records of the establishments of the Roman Catholic missionaries, whose faith and fervor enabled them to combat the difficulties around them in life, or to triumph over them in death.

By the operation of these causes, a knowledge of the great features of the continent was gradually acquired and the circle of French power and influence enlarged. As early as 1632, seven years only after the foundations of Quebec were laid, the missionaries had penetrated to Lake Huron, by the route of Grand River, and Father Sagard has left an interesting narrative of their toils and sufferings, upon its bleak and sterile shores. The Wyandots had been driven into that region, from the banks of the St. Lawrence, by their inveterate enemies the Iroquois, whose valor, and enterprise, and success constitute the romance of Indian history. The good priests accompanied them in this expatriation, and if they could not prevent their sufferings, they shared them. No portion of these wide domains was secure from the conquering Iroquois, and they pursued their discomfitted enemies with relentless fury. Little would be gained by an attempt to describe the events of this exterminating warfare. The details are as afflicting, as any recorded in the long annals of human vengeance and human sufferings. Villages were sacked; men, women and children murdered; and by day and by night, in winter and in summer, there was neither rest nor safety for the vanquished. The character of the missionaries did not exempt them from a full participation in the misfortunes of their converts, and many of them were murdered at the foot of the altar, with the crucifix in their hands, and the name of God upon their lips. Some were burned at the stake, with all those horrible accompaniments of savage ingenuity, which add intensity to the pangs of the victims, and duration to their sufferings.— But nothing could shake the fortitude of these apostles of benevolence. They lived the life of saints, and died the death of Martyrs. The feeble remnant of the once powerful Wyandots sought and found refuge among the Sioux, in the country west of Lake Superior. Here they remained, until the power of their enemies was reduced by their contests with the French when they descended the Upper Lakes and established themselves in this quarter.

It is now difficult to conceive, what however is well authenticated, that a century and a half ago, the great central point of Indian influence and intelligence was upon the southern shore of Lake Superior, and far towards its western extremity. This was the seat of the Chippewa power, and here was burning that eternal fire, whose extinction foretold, if it did not occasion, some great national calamity. No fact is better established in the whole range of Indian history than the devotion of some, if not all the tribes, to this characteristic feature of the ancient superstition of the Magi.— And it proves their separation from the primitive stock at an early day, when this belief was prevalent among the eastern nations. All the ceremonies, attending the preservation of this fire yet live in Indian tradition, and it was still

burning, when the French first appeared among them.—
There were male and female guardians, to whose care it
was committed; and when we recollect the solemn and
ritual and dreadful imprecations, with which the same pledge
of Roman safety was guarded and preserved, it ought not to
surprise us, that such importance was attached by the Indians to the ceaseless endurance of this visible emblem of
power, whose duration was to be co-eval with their national
existence. The augury has proved but too true. The
fire is extinct, and the power has departed from them. We
have trampled on the one and overthrown the other.

The circumstances of another custom have survived the
general wreck in which so much of their tradition has perished. Upon the Sandusky river, and near where the town
of Lower Sandusky now stands, lived a band of the
Wyandots, called the Neutral Nation. They occupied two
villages, which were cities of refuge, where those who
sought safety never failed to find it. During the long and
disastrous contests, which preceded and followed the arrival
of the Europeans, and in which the Iroquois contended for
victory, and their enemies for existence, this little band preserved the integrity of their territories, and the sacred character of peace-makers. More fortunate than the English
monarch, who seated upon the shore of the ocean, commanded its waves to come no farther, they stayed the troubled waters, which flowed around but not over them. All,
who met upon their threshold, met as friends, for the ground
on which they stood was holy. It was a beautiful institution; a calm and peaceful island, looking out upon a world
of waves and tempests. (1)

As the course of the French trade first took the route of
the Ottawas river, their establishments upon the Upper
Lakes preceded their settlements on our strait. Soon after

B

the middle of the seventeenth century, trading posts were established at Michilimackinac, at the Sault Ste Marie, at Green Bay, at Chicago, and at St. Joseph. It was soon known, from the reports of the Indians, that a great river flowed through the country beyond the Lakes in a southerly direction, and it became an object with the French authorities to ascertain its source, its outlet and its features.— Joliet, an inhabitant of Quebec, and Farther Marquette, were employed by the French Intendant to prosecute this discovery. They ascended the Fox river, crossed the Portage, descended the Ouisconsin, and entered the Mississippi, the 17th of June, 1673. They followed the current to the Arkansas river, when they were induced by untoward circumstances to return, leaving unsolved, the great question of the place of discharge of this mighty stream, where it was supposed the French interests would require a powerful and permanent establishment. They returned by the Illinois and re-entered Lake Michigan at Chicago.

The full completion of this discovery was reserved for, La Sale. He was a man of genius and cultivated talents. Firm in his resolutions, persevering in his efforts, full of recourse he seemed destined to enlarge the geographical knowledge, and to extend the dominion of his countrymen. He built the first vessel that ever navigated these Lakes.— She was launched at Erie, and called the Griffin. La Sale embarked in her, with every thing necessary for the prosecution of his undertaking, and in 1679, ascended this river. He reached Michilimackinac, where he left his vessel, and coasted along Lake Michigan in canoes, to the mouth of the St. Joseph. The Griffin was despatched to Green Bay for a cargo of furs, but she was never more heard of, after leaving that place. Whether she was wrecked, or captured and destroyed by the Indians, no one knew at that day, and none can tell now. La Sale prosecuted his enterprise with great vigor amid the most discouraging circumstances. By the abilities he displayed, by the successful result of his undertaking, and by the melancholy catastrophe, which terminated his own career, he is well worthy a place, among that band of intripid adventurers, who, commencing with Columbus, and terminating with Parry and Franklin, have devoted themselves with nobler ardor, to the extension of geographical knowledge, and have laid open the recesses of this continent. Among these, there is none, whose bearing was more lofty, or whose adventures, even now, excite a more thrilling interest, than those of Robert de La Sale. Time will not allow us to trace the incidents of his expedition. It is enough to observe, that he reached the Gulf of Mexico and saw the mingling of the great waters. From that time the French government conceived the splendid project of establishing a cordon of posts from Quebec, along these lakes and rivers, to the Delta of the Mississippi, by which the Indian tribes might be overawed, the fur trade secured and the colonies of their rival confined within comparative narrow limits. This plan was matured and in the process of rapid execution, before it attracted the attention of the British government. Our own Washington commenced his eventful public life, by an embassy to the commanding officers of the French posts upon the Ohio and Alleghany, remonstrating against their advancing establishments; and his journal evinces the sagacity with which he foresaw their plan, and its consequences. How different might have been the destiny of our country, had this scheme been accomplished.

It is difficult, at this day, to trace the causes of the attachment and aversion, which were respectively manifested by the various tribes, for the French and English. The interest of the former generally predominated, and they seem to have had a peculiar facility in identifying themselves with the feelings of the Indians, and in gaining their affections. But even in this quarter, the seeds of dissatisfaction were early sown, and ripened, as we shall see into an abundant harvest.— The Fox or Ottagami Indians, who then occupied this strait, evinced a restless disposition from their first acquaintance with the French, and determined predilection for the English. This was cultivated by the usual interchange of messages and presents, and an English trading expedition actually reached Michilimackinac in 1686.

During such a contest for supramacy, both in power and commerce, the great advantages, offered by an establishment upon this river, could not escape the observation of the contending parties. In fact, it is difficult to conceive, why it was so long postponed, and we can only account for it by recollecting, that the French had another and safer way, by which they could communicate with the northwestern regions. If the English entered the country at all, they must enter by this route, and a position here, was in fact the key of the whole region above us. Influenced by these motives, the English government seriously contemplated its occupation, but they were anticipated by the decisive movement of their rivals. A great Council was convened at Montreal, at which were present all the distinguished Chiefs of the various tribes occupying the country from Quebec to the Mississippi. It is described by the French historians, as the most numerous and imposing assemblage, ever collected around one council fire, and it was attended by the Governor-general, and all that was noble and powerful in New France. Its discussions, and proceedings, and results were fully recorded, and have come down to us unimpared. The whole policy of the French intercourse with the Indians was considered, and the wants and the complaints of the various parties made known. The Iroquois stated, that they had understood the French General was about to establish a post upon the Detroit river, and objected strenuously to the measure, because the country was theirs, and they had already prevented the English from adopting the same step. The Governor-general, in answer, informed them, that neither the Iroquois nor the English could claim the country, but that it belonged to the King of France; and that an expedition, destined for this service had already commenced its march. And we collect from the narrative of the proceedings, that in June, 1701, Mons. de la Motte Cadillac, with one hundred men and a Jesuit, left Montreal carrying with them every thing necessary for the commencement and support of an establishment, and reached this place in the month of July, one hundred and twenty-nine years since.

Hence then, commences the history of Detroit, and with it, the history of the Peninsula of Michigan. How numerous and diversified are the incidents, compressed within the period of its existence! No place in the United States presents such a series of events, interesting in themselves, and permanently affecting, as they occurred, its progress and prosperity. Five times its flag has changed, three different sovereignties have claimed its allegiance, and since it has been held by the United States, its government has been thrice transferred; twice it has been besieged by the Indians, once captured in war, and once burned to the ground. Identified as we are with its future fate, we may indulge the hope, that its chapter of accidents has closed, and that its advancement will be hereafter uninterrupted.

We have nowhere a connected account of the progress of this colony; occasional notices are interspersed through the French historians, and detailed descriptions are given of a few of the more important events; but the whole subject is involved in much obscurity. The statistical facts are altogether neglected. We have no comparative estimates of population or production; none of those severe investigations into the character and condition of the country which render modern history so valuable and satisfactory. A small stockaded fort was erected, extending from the present arsenal to Griswold street, and enclosing a few houses occupied by the persons attached to the post and the traders. The whole establishment was slight and rude, intended rather to overawe than seriously to resist the Indians. Only the third year after the position was taken, the Indians in its vicinity were invited to Albany, and many of the Chiefs of the Ottawas actually visited that place. They returned, disaffected to the French interest, and persuaded that the post was established here to restrain and eventually to subdue them. They set fire to the town, but it was fortunately discovered and extinguished before much injury was done. In the same spirit, and about the same time, a war party, on their return from a successful expedition against the Iroquois, paraded in front of the Fort, and attempted to induce the other Indians to join them in an attack. Monsieur de Tonte, who then held the command, detached the Sieur de Vincennes to repulse them. That officer executed the duty with so much valor and ability, that the Ottawas were defeated, and in their precipitate flight abandoned their prisoners, who fell into the hands of the French, and were restored to their countrymen.

At that time there were three villages in the vicinity of the Fort. One was a Huron village, the site of which was upon the farm now owned by Col. Jones. Another was a Potawatamie village upon the farm of Mr. Navarre, and the third was a village of the Ottawas, on the opposite shore and above the town. These were permanently occupied, but great numbers occasionally resorted here; and it was evident from many circumstances that the country was populous and the people well supplied. Charlevoix, who visited it in 1721, represents it as the most desirable part of New France. Game was abundant, and herds of buffalo were then ranging upon the prairies about the River Raisin.

The first serious calamity which threatened the infant colony with destruction, arose from an unexpected quarter. Until this time the Ottagamies or Foxes were little known, and no striking event had directed the attention of the French towards them. We are therefore unable to trace the causes which induced them to take up arms, or the means they had provided for the accomplishment of their daring enterprise. They appear to have been connected with the Iroquois, and with them to have embraced the English interest. Their history, for fifty years succeeding this period, is a history of desperate efforts, directed against the French and many of the tribes around them, evincing a firmness of purpose, a reckless valor, and a patient endurance of misfortunes, worthy of a better cause and a better fate.

In May, 1712, they determined to destroy the town, and, in conformity with the usual tactics of the Indians, to make their arrangements secretly, and to execute them suddenly. Under various pretences, they collected in the neighborhood in great numbers. Du Buisson was then the French commandant, and his garrison consisted of but twenty soldiers. The Ottawas, Wyandots, and Potawatamies, upon whose friendship and assistance he could rely were absent from their villages, engaged in hunting. An Ottagamie, who was a Christian convert, disclosed the plot to surprise him, before it was ripe for execution, and he took immediate measures to counteract it. Expresses were sent to call his allies to his assistance, and preparations were made for a vigorous defence. The Ottagamies, finding their object discovered commenced the attack, but on the 13th of May the French were greeted with the sight of a powerful body of their friends, naked, painted, and prepared for battle. The gates of the Fort were immediately opened to them, and they entered the council house, where in a confederacy with Du Buisson, they professed their attachment to the French, and their determination to defend them. They were received and answered as their professions and services well merited.

In the mean time, the Ottagamies had retreated to an entrenched camp they had previously formed where Jefferson Avenue intersects the eastern boundary of the city. Here they were invested by the allied forces, and a blockhouse was erected overlooking the defences of the Ottagamies, from which so severe a fire was kept up that they could not procure water. Their provisions were soon consumed, and hunger and thirst reduced them to extremity. Despair, however, invigorated them; and becoming the assailants, they succeeded in gaining possession of a house adjoining the Fort. They strengthened this new position and annoyed their adversaries. They were at length dislodged by the cannon, and driven back to their entrenchments.

At this time they made a pacific effort to terminate hostilities, and with this view a deputation was sent to Du Buisson. No confidence, however, being placed in their declarations, either by the French or Indians, their offer was rejected. When the deputation reported the result to the warriors, their indignation excited them to renewed and desperate efforts, and not less than three hundred arrows with lighted matches attached to them were discharged at the Fort. The houses were generally thatched with straw, and several of them were burned. The others were preserved by covering them with wet skins.

This determined resistance almost discouraged the French

commander. He seriously contemplated evacuating his post, and retiring to Michilimackinac. He convened his allies and disclosed his intention. They remonstrated against this measure, and promised to redouble their efforts. The war-song was again sung, and the parties repaired to their posts. The attack was so vigorous that the Ottagamies were reduced to extremity. Many of their bravest chiefs were killed, and their Fort was filled with the dying and the dead. They again demanded a parley, and the negociations were renewed. While these were pending, on the nineteenth day of the siege, a tremendous storm arose, and during the night they abandoned their fort without discovery, and with their women and children fled to the peninsula which advances into Lake St. Clair. Here they were pursued, and being incautiously attacked, the allies were repulsed with considerable loss. Four days were occupied in efforts to carry this new position, and on the fifth they succeeded, by means of a field battery erected by the French. The assailants entered the works in arms, and put to death almost all who had been opposed to them. The women and children were spared, and divided as slaves among the confederated tribes. The Ottagamies lost more than a thousand warriors in this disastrous expedition.

The subsequent fate of this tribe is not unworthy of notice. They collected their scattered bands, and established themselves on Fox River. But the same restless and reckless disposition accompanied them. Like the son of Hagar, their hand was against every man and every man's hand was against them. They commanded the communication between the Lakes and the Mississippi, so that it could only be traversed by large bodies of armed men. Their war parties were sent out in all directions and they kept the whole region in a continued state of alarm and danger. Their hostile attitude so seriously menaced the

French interest in that quarter, that an expedition was prepared and detached to subdue them. It was accompanied by the warriors of all the other tribes, who had been provoked to take signal vengeance by their fierce and troubled spirit.

The Ottagamies had selected a strong position upon the Fox River, since called Butte des Morts, or the Hill of the Dead, which they had fortified by three rows of palisades and a ditch. They here secured their women and children, and prepared for a vigorous defence. Their entrenchment was so formidable that De Louvigny the French commander declined an assault, and invested the place in form. By regular approaches, he gained a proper distance for mining their works, and was preparing to blow up one of the curtains, when they proposed a capitulation. Terms were eventually offered and accepted; and those who survived the siege were preserved and liberated. But the power of the tribe was broken, and their pride humbled. And, since this period, no remarkable incident has occurred in their history.

From 1720 to 1760 solitary facts in the history of Detroit may be here and there gleaned, but no continuous account can be given of its condition and progress. The materials are too scanty for unbroken narrative. It struggled with all the difficulties incident to a remote and exposed position. The savages around, although not often in open hostility, were vindictive and treacherous; and no one could tell when or how they might attack it. In 1749, considerable additions were made to the settlements upon the river, and emigrants were sent out at the expense of the government, supplied with farming utensils, provisions, and other means of support. The continued wars between France and England, which filled so large a portion of the eighteenth century, extended their influence to this quarter, and a company of militia detailed from the inhabitants, and commanded by an ancestor of one of our most respectable families, that of Campau, fought in the great battle where Braddock was defeated and killed. But it was under the walls of Quebec that the fate of this country was decided. Upon the plains of Abraham the victor and the vanquished poured out their blood together, displaying in death, as they had displayed in life, traits of magnanimity and heroism worthy of the best days of chivalry. "Who flies?" said the expiring Wolfe, to an exclamation of one of the mourning group around him. He was answered, "The enemy!" "Then" said he "I die happy,"—and he died. His fate so picturesque and glorious, recalls the memory of Epaminondas and Gustavus, upon the plains of Mantinea and Lutzen.— Victory crowned their standards and death sealed their career. His rival in fame, and in all but fortune, Montcalm, nobly supported the honor of France, and fell too soon for his country, though too late for himself. But a few brief years afterwards, and another noble and gallant leader attempted to plant the standard of freedom upon the rocky battlements of Quebec. He fell, where Wolfe and Montcalm had fallen before him, but the memory of Montgomery will be cherished, as long as the sacred cause, for which he fought and died.

In 1760, the British under the capitulation of Montreal, took possession of Detroit and the upper posts, and in 1763, these were finally ceded by France. At this period, the French had establishments at St. Joseph, at Green Bay, at Michilimackinac, at Detroit, at the Maumee and Sandusky. As fortifications, most of these were slight and unimportant, intended rather as depots of trade, than as military establishments. The positions were selected with much judgment and knowledge of the country, and they yet command the great avenues of communication to the world of woods and waters beyond us. In succeeding however to the power, it was soon found, that the English had not succeeded to the interest and influence of the French. Whatever may have been the cause, the fact is certain, that there is in the French character, a peculiar adaptation to the habits and feelings of the Indians, and to this day, the period of French domination is the era of all that is happy in Indian reminiscence.

No sooner had the English obtained possession of the country, than a spirit of disaffection became visible, which extended to all the tribes in this region, and finally led to the conception and execution of a plan, equally able and daring for their overthrow.

There was then upon the stage of action, one of those high and heroic men, who stamp their own characters upon the age, in which they live, and who appear destined to survive the lapse of time, like some proud and lofty column, which sees, crumbling around it, the temples of God, and the dwellings of man, and yet rests upon its pedestal, time worn, but time honored. This man was at the head of the Indian confederacy, and had acquired an influence over his countrymen, such has had never before been seen, and such as we may not expect to see again. To form a just estimate of his character, we must judge him by the circumstances in which he was placed; by the profound ignorance and barbarism of his people; by his own destitution of all education and information, and by the jealous, fierce and intractable spirit of his compeers. When measured by this standard, we shall find few of the men, whose names are familiar to us, more remarkable for all they proposed and achieved, than Pontiac. Were his race destined to endure, until the mists of antiquity could gather round his days and deeds, tradition would dwell upon his feats, as it has done in the old world, upon all who, in the infancy of nations, have been prominent actors for evil or for good. Pontiac was an Ottawa, and had been a celebrated and successful warrior.

His virtues seem to have been his own, and his vices, those of his age and nation. Major Rogers, who conducted to Detroit the first British detachment, was met upon his route by Pontiac and his warriors. He states that the chief sent to demand why he entered his country, and informed him that he stood in the path, and that the troops could not proceed, until their objects were satisfactorily explained. At an interview between them, the British commander assured him, his object was not to claim the country, but to remove from it the French troops, who had prevented a friendly intercourse between the English and the Indians. Proper belts were interchanged, and the desired permission was given — Pontiac accompanied them, and by his authority prevented an attack, which was meditated, at the mouth of the river. Major Rogers states, that during the subsequent operations of Pontiac, he issued a currency, which was received by the French settlers and faithfully redeemed by him. These bills of credit were drawn upon bark, and represented the article which had been delivered to him, and were authenticated by the figure of an otter, the totem of his family.— If Rogers has given a faithful narrative of his proceedings, his arrangements were combined with skill and judgment and his designs prosecuted with great inflexibility of purpose, and a daring, yet cool and tempered courage. We are no where told the causes of disaffection, which separated him from the British interest, and in fact, we have no regular history of the remarkable occurrences upon this frontier, which accompanied and followed his enterprise. A manuscript journal has been preserved, which records the more prominent facts, but it is a crude and ill digested memoir, dilating upon unimportant topics, and beneath criticism as a composition. Unfortunately too, it is mutilated, and the narrative terminates in the middle of the battle of Bloody-bridge. All the cotemporaneous relations, it has been recently possible to procure, have been recorded, and upon these we must principally rely for a connected narrative of the most extraordinary effort made by the Indians to take signal vengeance upon their oppressors, since the discovery of the continent. (Note II.)

Pontiac meditated a sudden and cotemporaneous attack upon the British posts on these Lakes, and upon the Forts at Niagara, Presqu'Isle, Le Bœuf, Venango, and Pittsburg. His design was to carry them by treachery, and to massacre their garrisons. He then intended to take possession of the country, and to oppose the introduction of any British force. He calculated, that these successes would give confidence to all the tribes, and unite them in a general confederacy.

His first object was to gain his own tribe, and the warriors, who generally attended him. Topics, to engage their attention and inflame their passions, could not be wanting.— A belt was exhibited, which he pretended to have received from the King of France, urging him to drive the British from the country, and to open the paths for the return of the French. The British troops had not endeavored to conciliate the Indians, and mutual causes of complaint existed. Some of the Ottawas had been disgraced by blows. But, above all, the British were intruders in the country, and would ere long conquer the Indians, as they had conquered the French, and wrest from them their lands.

After these topics had been skillfully managed, a great council was convened at the River Aux Ecorces, when Pontiac addressed the Indians with equal eloquence and effect. He called to his aid their prevalent superstition, and related a dream, in which the Great Spirit had recently disclosed to a Delaware Indian, the conduct he expected his red children to pursue. I shall not occupy your time by a recital of the various circumstances, attending the translation of this seer, from earth to heaven. They were distinctly narrated by Pontiac, and such is the effect of superstition upon the human mind, that they were perhaps related with as much good faith, as they were received. In the interview between the Great Spirit and his chosen minister to the Indians, minute instructions were given for their conduct in this, the peculiar crisis of their fate. They were directed to abstain from ardent spirits, and to cast from them the manufactures of the white man. To resume their bows and arrows, and the skins of the animals for clothing. "And why," said the Great Spirit, indignantly to the Delaware, "why do you suffer these dogs in red clothing to enter your country, and take the land I gave you?" "Drive them from it, and when you are in distress, I will help you!"

The speech of Pontiac, and the dream of the Delaware, produced a powerful effect upon the wild and reckless multitude, who eagerly listened to the tale of their wrongs, and the offer of revenge. A plan of operation was concerted, and belts and speeches were sent to secure the co-operation of the Indians, along the whole line of the frontier.

In the month of May 1763, the preparatory arrangements having been completed, the Indians commenced a sudden and simultaneous attack upon each of the twelve British posts, extending from Niagara to Green Bay in the northwest, and to Pittsburgh in the south-west. So well had their measures been taken, and so secretly guarded, that the storm burst upon the garrisons, before they had time to learn the intentions of their enemies; much less to prepare for them. And a more signal proof cannot be given, of the deep and deadly feeling of the Indians, and of the influence exercised over them by Pontiac, than is furnished by the progress of this enterprise. In a period of profound peace, and along a line of frontier extending a thousand miles, and secured upon all the important points by fortified posts, simultaneous attacks were made without the slightest suspicion being excited on the part of the British. Nine of these posts were captured. The circumstances attending the surprise of Michilimackinac are better known than those, which led to the success of the Indians at any other place. The Fort was then upon the main land, near the northern point of the peninsula. The Ottawas, to whom the assault was committed, prepared for a great game of ball, to which the officers were invited. While engaged in play, one of the parties gradually inclined towards the Fort, and the other pressed after them. The ball was once or twice thrown over the pickets, and the Indians were suffered to enter and procure it. Almost all the garrison were present as spectators, and those upon duty were negligent and unprepared. Suddenly, the ball was again thrown into the Fort, and all the Indians rushed after it. The rest of the tale is soon told. The troops were butchered, and the Fort destroyed.

Niagara and Pittsburgh were regular fortifications.—They were invested by the Iroquois, but the attempt to subdue them was unsuccessful. It does not fall within the task I have assigned to myself, to relate the circumstances of their danger and relief. They were both too important to be neglected; and Pittsburgh was saved by the expedition of Boquet, who dispersed the besiegers at the point of the bayonet.

Upon the possession of Detroit, however, depended in the opinion of the Indians the ultimate issue of their project.—Its capture would release the French inhabitants of the strait, from their temporary allegiance to the British, and would unite their line of operations by this connecting link. Its reduction, therefore, was undertaken by Pontiac in person.

The half bastioned work which has been recently demolished was not at this period erected. That was projected and completed during our revolutionary war, when an attack was apprehended from the struggling colonies. And this apprehension was not without cause, for as early as 1776, Congress, in secret session, directed the plan of an expedition against Fort Detroit, and an estimate of the expense, to be prepared and submitted to them. And, on a subsequent day, this inquiry was extended to the necessary means for securing the naval ascendancy upon Lake Erie. The expedition, however, was not undertaken. The pressure of more immediate danger, probably withdrew the attention of Congress from so remote and doubtful an enterprise.

We may infer from the diary, which has been preserved, of the occurrences of the siege, and from the traditionary descriptions, which can be collected, that the town was enclosed by a single row of pickets, forming nearly the four sides of a square. That there were block-houses at the corners and over the gates, and that an open space, called the Chemin du Ronde, intervened between the houses and the pickets, forming a place of arms, encircling the town. The fortifications did not extend to the river, and during the siege, all the gates were closed, except the water gate, which opened towards the stream. Two armed vessels were anchored in front of the town, and formed an important portion of its defences. One of these was the Beaver. The name of the other, I have not been able to obtain. There were in the Fort two six pounders, one three pounder, and three mortars. But they were badly mounted, and rather calculated to terrify, than to annoy the Indians. Major Gladwyn had superceded Major Campbell, a few days before, in the command, and the garrison consisted of one hundred and twenty-two men, and eight officers. To these were added forty traders and engagées, who resided in the town. I cannot ascertain, that there was any immediate want of provisions or ammunition.

Such was the relative situation of the British and Indians, when Pontiac, having completed his arrangements, on the 8th of May, 1763, presented himself at the gates of the town, with a considerable body of his warriors, and requested a council with the commanding officer. His plan was well devised, and had it been secretly kept, must have been successful. The Indians had sawed off their rifles so short, as to conceal them under their blankets. One of our most intelligent French inhabitants, Col. Beaufait, has informed me, that his father, returning that day from the Fort, met Pontiac and his party upon Bloody Bridge. The last warrior was his particular friend, and as he passed him, he threw aside his blanket, and exhibited the shortened rifle, intimating, at the same time, the project they had in view. The Indian Chief intended to meet the British commander in council, and at a given signal, which was to be the presentation of a belt of wampum in a particular manner, his attendants were to massacre all the officers, and rushing to the gates, to open them, and admit the warriors, who were to be ready on the out side, for immediate entrance. An indiscriminate slaughter was to follow, together with the demolition of the fort, and the annihilation of the British power.

How Major Gladwyn acquired a knowledge of this atrocious scheme cannot now be ascertained. The accounts, which have been given of its disclosure, are at variance, and it is possible, that that officer may not have revealed the secret, from well founded apprehensions of the consequences to his friendly monitor. I am inclined to believe that an Indian woman, named Catherine, who was frequently employed in making moccasins for the garrison, was the person, who communicated the important information. It is said, that she had previously completed a number of pair for Major Gladwyn, and had been so well rewarded, that her gratitude was excited. On the evening preceding the day assigned by the Indians for the catastrophe, an elk skin was delivered to her, for the purpose of making some very fine moccasins. After receiving it, she lingered about the quarters of the commanding officer, as though unwilling to depart, and when urged to leave the Fort before the gates were closed, she gave some equivocal answer, and requested to be led to Major Gladwyn. She then disclosed the whole plan. It was fortunate that her warning was well received. Major Gladwyn employed the night in making the necessary preparations. His defences were strengthened, his arms and ammunition examined and arranged, and every man within the fort, civil and military, was directed to be ready for instant and urgent service. The officers walked upon the ramparts during the night, not certain, but that the usual inconstancy of the Indians might precipitate their movements, and urge an immediate assault. All, however, was silent, except the songs and dances in the Indian camps, which alone broke upon the stillness of the night. They employed the time, as they usually do, upon the eve of any great enterprise, in singing and dancing, anticipating the full success of their scheme.

In the morning, Pontiac and his warriors sang their war song, danced their war dance, and repaired to the Fort. They were admitted without hesitation, and were conducted to the council house, where Major Gladwyn and his officers were prepared to receive them. They perceived at the gate, and as they passed through the streets, an unusual activity and movement among the troops. The garrison was under arms, the guards were doubled, and the officers were armed with swords and pistols. Pontiac inquired of the British commander, what was the cause of this unusual appearance. He was answered, that it was proper to keep the young men to their duty, lest they should become idle and ignorant. The business of the council then commenced, and Pontiac proceeded to address Major Gladwyn. His speech was bold and menacing, and his manner and gesticulations vehement, and they became still more so, as he approached the critical moment. When he was upon the point of presenting the belt to Major Gladwyn, and all was breathless expectation, the drums, at the door of the council house, suddenly rolled the charge, the guards levelled their pieces, and the British officers drew their swords from their scabbards. Pontiac was a brave man, constitutionally and habitually. He had fought in many a battle, and often led his warriors to victory. But this unexpected and decisive proof, that his treachery was discovered and prevented, entirely disconcerted him. Tradition says he trembled. And at all events, he delivered his belt in the usual manner, and thus failed to give his party the concerted signal of attack. Major Gladwyn immediately approached the chief, and drawing aside his blanket, discovered the shortened rifle, and then, after stating his knowledge of the plan, and reproaching him for his treachery, ordered him from the Fort. The Indians immediately retired, and as soon as they had passed the gate, they gave the yell, and fired upon the garrison. They then proceeded to the commons, where was living an aged English woman with her two sons. These, they murdere and then repaired to Hog Island, where a discharged serjeant resided with his family, who were all but one, immediately massacred. Thus was the war commenced.

There were several buildings surrounding the Fort, and but a short distance from it. Behind these, and the picket fences, the Indians stationed themselves, and commenced a violent fire upon the British. This was returned; but such was the situation of both parties, that little injury was done. The firing however was continued for some days, the Indians anticipating much more serious effects from these attacks, than were actually experienced by their enemies. The British commander was ignorant of the system of tactics, which teaches the Indians to consider the sacrifice of human life as dishonorable, and the weakness of his defences led him to fear an assault. Believing his position in such an event would be untenable, preparations were made for an immediate embarkation on board the vessels, and a retreat to Niagara. The positive assurances, however, of the principal French inhabitants, that so hazardous a measure would never be adopted by the Indians, re-assured him, and in the course of a few days, all the erections without the Fort, which could afford security to the besiegers, were burned, either by hot shot, or by sorties, which were made by the garrison. The Indians could then only annoy the Fort, by approaching the summit of a low ridge, which overlooked the pickets, where they continued their fire from time to time.

Major Campbell, who had been superceded by Major Gladwyn, still remained in the Fort. He had held the command since the surrender of the country, and was well known to the Indians. He seems to have exercised his authority moderately and wisely, and was esteemed both by them and the Canadians. Pontiac conceived the design of getting this officer into his possession, and holding him as a pledge for the surrender of the Fort. For this purpose, he requested some of the French inhabitants, who were the means of communication between the British and the Indians, to inform Major Campbell he wished an interview with him at his camp, that they might terminate the present difficulties, and smoke the pipe of peace together. He promised solemnly, that Major Campbell should be permitted to go and come in perfect safety. Messrs. Godfroy and Chapoton, who had visited him on this occasion, were deceived by his professions and promises, and advised Maj. Campbell to meet him. Such was the anxiety of all to bring to a conclusion this irksome warfare, that this officer, accompanied by Lieut. McDougall, repaired to Pontiac's camp, in the hope of making a satisfactory arrangement with him. They were at first well received; but without entering into the details of the story, it is sufficient to observe, that they were ultimately detained, and held as hostages. Pontiac offered Major Campbell's life for the surrender of the Fort, apparently not aware, that one violation of good faith must destroy all confidence between contending parties, and that in this case, any sudden impulse might lead to the massacre of the garrison, as easily as it had led to the detention of Major Campbell.

The melancholy fate of this self-devoted officer adds another to the many proofs, which our intercourse with Indians has furnished, of the little confidence to be placed in their promises, made in the excitement of war. Major Campbell and Lieut. McDougall were detained at the house of Mr. Meloche, at Bloody Bridge. They were allowed occasionally to walk out, but the Indians were so numerous around, that escape was difficult and hazardous. Lieut. McDougal, however, proposed to his fellow prisoner to make the attempt, but as his vision was very imperfect, he declined, that he might not impede the flight of his friend. McDougal reached the Fort in safety. During one of the sorties made by the British, an Ottawa Chief, of some distinction, from Michilimackinac, was killed. His nephew, who was present, determined upon revenge, hastened instantly to Bloody Bridge, where he found Major Campbell walking in the road. He approached and struck him dead with his tomahawk. He then fled to Saginaw, apprehensive of the vengeance of Pontiac; and it is but justice to the memory of that chief to say, that he was indignant at this attrocious act, and used every exertion to apprehend the murderer, who would, no doubt, have paid with his life, for his temerity.

On the 21st of May, the small vessel was dispatched to Niagara, to hasten the arrival of the reinforcement, and the provisions and ammunition which were expected for the place; and on the 30th, the sentinel on duty announced, that a fleet of boats was coming round the point, at the Huron church. The whole garrison flocked to the bastions, eagerly anticipating the arrival of their friends. But they were greeted with no sounds of joy. The death-cry of the Indians, that harbinger of misery, alone broke upon the ear. The fate of the detachment was at once known. The Indians had ascertained their approach and had stationed a party of warriors at Point Pelée. Twenty-three batteaux, laden with all the stores necessary for the defence of the town, and the subsistence of the garrison, and manned by a detachment of troops, landed at this place in the evening, ignorant of danger, and unsuspicious of attack. The enemy watched all their movements, and about the dawn of day, rushed upon them. An officer, with thirty men, threw himself into a boat, and crossed the lake, to Sandusky Bay. All the others were killed or taken. The line of barges ascended the river on the opposite shore, escorted by the Indians upon the bank, and guarded by detachments in each boat, in full view of the garrison, and of the whole French settlement. The prisoners were compelled to navigate the boats. As the first batteaux arrived opposite to the town, four British soldiers determined to effect their liberation, or to perish in the attempt. They suddenly changed the course of the boat, and by loud cries made known their intention to the crew of the vessel.

The Indians in the other boats, and the escort upon the bank, fired upon the fugitives, but they were soon driven from their positions by a cannonade from the armed schooner. The guard on board this boat leaped overboard, and one of them dragged a soldier with him into the water, where both were drowned. The others escaped to the shore, and the boat reached the vessel, with another soldier wounded. Lest the other prisoners might escape, they were immediately landed, and marched up the shore, to the lower point of Hog Island, where they crossed the river, and were immediately put to death with all the horrible accompaniments of savage cruelty.

On the third of June, the important information of a peace between France and England, and of the cession of the country to the latter, reached the Fort. It was immediately communicated to the French inhabitants, who found their position essentially changed by this measure. Until now, they were prisoners upon capitulation; a neutral party between the belligerents. They had conducted with the most exemplary fidelity, and during the whole seige, very few Canadians were known to have connected themselves with the Indians, and these were held in abhorrence by their countrymen, and were compelled by their indignation, eventually to flee, and seek shelter in Illinois. The operations of the war had pressed heavily upon them. At first, their cattle were killed and provisions taken, whenever a hungry or drunken party chose to distress them. Pontiac soon became satisfied, that this indiscriminate plunder would leave the French people, as well as his own, without the means of support, and contributions were afterwards regularly levied, and supplies furnished, through a commissariat department, instituted by him. Finding, however, that his means were inadequate to the reduction of the Fort, he assembled the principal French inhabitants in

Council, and in the presence of all his warriors, presented them with a war-belt, and told them, if they were French they would accept it, if they were English, he would make war upon them. One of the principal inhabitants was appointed by the others to speak for them, and he exhibited the articles of peace between the French and British governments, and said to Pontiac, " My brother; you see that our arms are tied by your great Father, the King: untie this knot, and we will join you. Till that is done, we shall sit quietly upon our mats." (Note III.) After much discussion, the assembly dispersed, without any satisfactory arrangement. And the French inhabitants resisted all the efforts of the Indians to induce them to unite with them. At this time, the vessel, which had been despatched to Niagara, arrived at the mouth of the river, with about sixty troops on board and a supply of provisions and ammunition. The wind was light and baffling, and the Indians made every effort to capture her. The warriors quit the siege, and repaired to Fighting Island, determined to board the vessel, as she ascended the river. I find no authority for the account usually given of the circumstances attending the attack of this vessel, or of the order given by her captain to blow her up, when the Indians were about to ascend her deck. She left the mouth of the river, where the Indians had annoyed her in their canoes, with a favorable breeze, which however failed, as she reached the point of Fighting Island, where she was compelled to anchor. The captain had concealed his men in the hold, so that the Indians were not aware of the strength of the crew. Soon after dark, they embarked in their canoes, and proceeded to board the vessel. The men were silently ordered up, and took their stations at the guns. The Indians were suffered to approach close to the vessel, when the captain, by

D

the stroke of a hammer upon the mast, which had been previously concerted, gave the signal for action. An immediate discharge took place, and the Indians precipitately fled, with many killed and wounded. The next morning, the vessel dropped down to the mouth of the river, where she remained six days waiting for a wind. On the thirtieth she succeeded in ascending the river, and reaching the Fort in safety.

Pontiac felt the necessity of destroying these vessels, and he therefore constructed rafts for that purpose. The barns of some of the inhabitants were demolished, and the materials employed in this work. Pitch and other combustables were added, and the whole so formed as to burn with rapidity and intensity. They were of considerable length, and were towed to a proper position, above the vessels, when fire was applied, and they were left to the stream, in the expectation, that they would be carried in contact with the vessels, and immediately set fire to them. Twice the attempt was made, and unsuccessful. The British were aware of the design, and took their measures accordingly. Boats were constructed, and anchored with chains above the vessels, and every precaution was used to ward off the blow. The blazing rafts passed harmlessly by, and other incidents soon occurred to engage the attention of the Indians. On the 29th of July, a fleet of boats was descried, ascending the river. Anxious to ascertain whether they had escaped the attacks of the Indians, a gun was fired from the Fort, which was immediately answered by the boats, each of which carried four swivels, and two mortars, and on board the whole, was a detachment of 300 regular troops, under the command of Captain Dalyell, an Aid-de-camp of Sir Jeffrey Amherst, the British Commander-in-Chief.

That evening arrangements were made for an attack

upon the Indian camp. Unfortunately, these were not so secretly conducted, but that information was conveyed to the Indians. Their women and children were immediately removed, and their plan of operations concerted. A party of warriors was stationed behind the pickets upon the farm now owned by Mr. Dequindre, and another party upon the farm at Bloody-bridge, protected by pickets and cord-wood, and concealed in the high grass. A detachment of three hundred men left the Fort, about an hour before day, and marched rapidly up the bank, expecting to surprise the Indians. They were suffered to reach the bridge over Bloody run, and to proceed about half way across it, before a gun was fired, or the slightest movement indicated, that the enemy was aware of their approach. Suddenly a volley was poured upon the troops who were thrown into instant confusion. They fought with the characteristic bravery of British soldiers, but the darkness of the night, the nature of an Indian attack, and the unfavorable position they occupied, rendered their fate critical and perilous. Capt. Dalyell fell at the first discharge, when the command devolved upon Captain Grant. The detachment was attacked upon the left flank, and upon the front and rear. Thus nearly surrounded, it was instantly perceived, that nothing but the most vigorous efforts could rescue them. It was necessary to drive the enemy from their positions, before a retreat could be undertaken. A charge was ordered, and it was promptly and vigorously effected. The Indians fell back before the bayonet, and were repulsed in every direction. The detachment extricated themselves from their perilous situation, and at length reached the Fort. They lost in this disastrous affair, seventy men killed, and forty wounded.

From this period, nothing important occurred in the prosecution of the siege. Pontiac, whether satisfied with the success he had gained, or discouraged by the defence of the place, relaxed in his efforts, and the Indians soon began to depart for their wintering grounds. All was quiet during the winter, and in the spring, the various bands as they arrived, professed their desire for peace. In the course of the season, General Bradstreet reached Detroit, with a well appointed army of three thousand men. Tradition says, that in passing the iron bound coast, west of Cleaveland, he encountered a violent storm, in which he lost a number of boats and many men. Certainly the imagination cannot conceive a more awful situation, than that of an army enclosed by a raging sea on one side, and an eternal rampart of rocks on the other. Low and feeble would be the sound of its cannon amid the roar of the elements around it. Mean and humble its proud banners, upon the crest of the billows. Nothing, and less than nothing, its strength before the power of the Almighty. Well may we exclaim in the language of Scripture, "Lord what is man that thou art mindful of him, or the son of man, that thou regardest him?"

General Bradstreet landed at Sandusky, and at the Maumee, and dispersed the Indians whom he found there, burning their villages, and destroying their cornfields. He reached Detroit without opposition. All the tribes in this region immediately visited him, and peace was firmly established. Pontiac, either distrusting the professions of the British, or too much exasperated to live cordially with them, declined any intercourse with their troops, and took no part in the pending negociations. He abandoned the country, and repaired to Illinois. Here, owing to some cause, which has not been explained, he was assassinated by a Peoria Indian. Such was the respect inspired by his talents and services, that the Ottawas, Potawattamies and Chippewas considered his death as a public misfortune, and its atonement, a sacred duty. They commenced a war upon the Peorias, in which that tribe was almost exterminated, and from which they never recovered. But a few families are now left to tell the tale of their misfortunes. The memory of the great Ottawa Chief is yet held in reverence among his countrymen, and whatever is the fate, which may await them, his name and deeds will live in their traditionary narratives, increasing in interest as they increase in years. (Note IV.)

A few years of tranquility succeeded these stormy events. They were employed by the British authorities in extending and consolidating their power, and by their citizens in a vigorous and profitable prosecution of the fur trade. The remote boundary of French enterprise was soon passed. The energy and activity of commerce and competition carried the adventurers to the arctic circle, seeking amid the ice and snows of a polar winter, those rich peltries, which nature has bestowed upon the north. It may be doubted, however, whether this traffic was permanently beneficial. Its products were subject to great fluctuations of value, depending not less upon the uncertain supply, than upon the caprice of fashion. And it withdrew, from the sober and safer pursuits of agriculture, the youth of the country—exchanging habits of steady industry, for those alternations of exertion and relaxation, which are equally pernicious to their constitution and their morals. No effort was made by the British government to promote the settlement of the country. A system of conciliation towards the Indians was adopted and persevered in; and in a few years, that bitter animosity, which was the fruit of a century of hostilities, gradually gave way, and they became firmly attached to the British interests.

But that great event was now approaching, which has

produced, and is yet destined to produce, such important changes in the moral and political state of the world. The contest between the mother country and her colonies soon absorbed all questions of minor interest, upon the continent; and the active employment of the Indian force became a favorite object in the British policy. Detroit, from its position, and from the associations of the Indians, was the controlling point of influence, where parties were organised and equipped, and whence they were despatched to lay waste our frontier, and to do the other nameless deeds of horror, which I am as unable to describe, as you would be unwilling to hear. It was a warfare to distress, not to subdue. He who has seen his family murdered in the darkness of the night, and by the light of his own dwelling, while he feels the pressure of his woe, feels, also, the desire of revenge, and the hope of attaining it.

I shall not dwell upon these attrocious scenes. War parties were going and returning, during the whole progress of the revolution. They went with presents and promises, and they returned with scalps and blood.

Two expeditions, however were undertaken, more important in their character and results, than the ordinary marauding enterprises, to which we have alluded. One of these was led by Capt. Byrd, whose force was composed of a detachment of regular troops, some militia, and a numerous body of Indian warriors. They left here in boats, well provided with provisions, and munitions of war. They ascended the Maumee, and descended the Miami river to the Ohio. The first object of the expedition was an attack upon Louisville, but the unusually wet season, and consequent high state of the water, induced him to ascend the Licking, and strike at the posts in the interior of Kentucky. With this view he appeared suddenly before Ruddle's station, and as he was supplied with cannon, and led a well appointed force, all hope of resistance was desperate, and the garrison surrendered upon promise of safety and protection from the Indians. It is needless to add, that the promise was utterly disregarded. Byrd proceeded a few miles further, and captured another small stockade, called Martin's station. His progress spread consternation through the country, and efforts were made to collect a force to oppose him. Before this could be organised, he suddenly abandoned his enterprise, and precipitately withdrew. His motives for this proceedure are unknown, whatever they may have been, Kentucky was relieved from the most imminent danger, to which she had ever been exposed.

George Rogers Clark was one of those men, who seemed born to conduct our country, through the troubled and dangerous scenes of the revolution. He possessed that quick perception, that instant decision, that fruitful resource, that power over others, and that confidence in himself, which constitute the great military leader. Whether the theatre of operations be great or small, an empire or an Indian frontier, the genius of such a man, must lead him to command, as surely as it will lead him to success.

Gen. Clark had been despatched by the Virginia government to defend the Kentucky frontier, then feeble and exposed. He soon became satisfied, that the most effectual means of attaining this object, was by capturing the British posts in the Illinois country. He accordingly descended the Ohio, and reduced Kaskaskia, Cahokia, and the small establishments in that quarter. When information of his success reached Detroit, Governor Hamilton resolved to dislodge him, and, for this purpose, collected all the regular troops, militia and Indians, who could be spared from the defence of this frontier. He proceeded to Vincennes and there halted, determined to attack his enemy, as soon as the season for field operations should commence. His plan was to regain the lost posts, and to destroy Clark's detachment; then to cross the Ohio, and sweep the infant settlements of Kentucky before him, giving up, to murder and devastation, the inhabitants and their property. But his design was anticipated and frustrated, by one of those bold and decisive movements, which marks the character of a general, and determines the fate of nations. Clark received information from a Spanish merchant, that his enemy was careless and secure, and had detached a part of his force to watch the Ohio river, and to harrass the frontiers. He immediately prepared a small armed boat, and put on board the supplies for his troops. He ordered her to proceed to the Wabash, and, taking post a few miles below Vincennes, to permit nothing to ascend or descend the river. He then, in the depth of winter, set out for that place, with his whole disposable force, amounting to only one hundred and thirty men. He was sixteen days crossing the country, and during five of these, he was employed in wading through the inundated prairies of the Wabash. For five miles, his detachment, marched with the water to their breasts. After surmounting these obstacles, he suddenly appeared before Vincennes, and by the stratagem of presenting a tree, shaped like a cannon, he pursuaded Hamilton, that he had brought artillery with him. His decisive movement, and the surprise and consternation of the enemy, led to the surrender of the Fort upon the first summons. Hamilton himself, and a few of those counsellors who had been most active in promoting his system of savage barbarities, were sent to Virginia in irons. The militia from this quarter were permitted to return.

The revolution terminated with the recognition of our independence. The subsequent events, in the history of the Territory are familiar to all of us. Difficulties soon arose respecting the surrender of the posts. An Indian war was the consequence, and the campaigns of Harmar, St. Clair and Wayne, were successively prosecuted before peace was established. The part taken by the British authorities here, to encourage the Indians in hostilities, and to aid their operations, are matters of history; and General Wayne, in the official report of his victory at the Maumee, states, that a company of militia from Detroit was associated with the Indians, and fought in their ranks. It is well known to the old inhabitants, that the clerk of the court, one Smith, was at the head of this company, and was killed in the action.

I have no pleasure in the retrospective view of these revolting scenes. But history is not the panegyric of human actions. It is our destiny to meet good and evil, in the chequered scenes of life. And it is our duty to draw lessons of instruction from the vices, as well as the virtues of our nature.

In the beginning of June, 1796, Capt. Porter, with a detachment of American troops, entered the Fort, which had been previously evacuated by the British. The American flag was displayed, and the dominion of the country peaceably transferred.

Without indulging in any presumptuous anticipations, we may hope, that the last change in our political condition has occurred, except that, which is to terminate our colonial situation, and to admit us, as an independent member of that great confederacy of republics, whose sway now extends from the lakes to the Gulf of Mexico, and from the Atlantic to the Pacific.

Wiser shall we be than the Roman people, and happier in our destiny, if we realize the truth so beautifully expressed by the greatest of their poets, and which is not less applicable to us, than to the Italian husbandmen,—

  Oh fortunatos nimiùm, sua si bona nôrint.

Fortunate indeed, if we appreciate the blessings of self-government, the value of our institutions, the moral, political and physical advantages we enjoy. The pariots of the revolution have passed or are passing away. They acquired, and have transmitted to us, the noblest system of government, which ever shed its blessings upon mankind. As it is the boast of every American, that he enjoys it; let it be his hope and effort, to transmit it, as a precious inheritance, unimpaired, to his posterity.

NOTES.

(I) PAGE 13.—This neutral nation, so called by Father Seguard, was still in existence two centuries ago, when the French missionaries first reached the Upper Lakes. The details of their history, and of their character and privileges, are meagre and unsatisfactory; and this is the more to be regretted, as such a sanctuary, among the barbarous tribes, is not only a singular institution, but altogether at variance with that reckless spirit of cruelty, with which their wars are usually prosecuted. The Wyandot tradition represents them, as having separated from the parent stock, during the bloody wars between their own tribe and the Iroquois, and having fled to the Sandusky river for safety. That they here erected two Forts, within a short distance of each other, and assigned one to the Iroquois, and the other to the Wyandots and their allies, where their war-parties might find security and hospitality, whenever they entered their country. Why so unusual a proposition was made, and acceded to, tradition does not tell. It is probable, however, that superstition lent its aid to the institution, and that it may have been indebted for its origin to the feasts, and dreams, and juggling ceremonies, which constituted the religion of the Aborigines. No other motive was sufficiently powerful to stay the hand of violence, and to counteract the threat of vengeance.

An intestine feud finally arose in this neutral nation, one party espousing the cause of the Iroquois, and the other of their enemies, and like most civil wars, this was prosecuted with relentless fury. Our informant says, that since his recollection, the remains of a red cedar post were yet to be seen where the prisoners were tied, previously to being burned.

(II) PAGE 26.—*Some account of a very remarkable North American Indian Chief; from Major Rogers' account of that country—lately published.*

The Indians on the lakes are generally at peace with one another, having a wide, extended and fruitful country in their possession. They are formed into a sort of empire, and the emperor is elected from the eldest tribe, which is the Ottawas, some of whom inhabit near our fort at Detroit, but are mostly westward toward the Mississippi. Pontiac is their present King, as emperor, who has certainly the largest empire and greatest authority of any Indian Chief that has appeared on the continent since our acquaintance with it. He puts on an air of majesty and princely grandeur, and is greatly honored and revered by his subjects. He not long since formed the design of uniting all the Indian nations together under his authority, but miscarried in the attempt.

In the year 1760 when I commanded and marched the first detachment into this country, that was ever sent there by the English, I was met in my way by an embassy sent from him, of some of his warriors, and some of the Chiefs of the tribes, that are under him: the purport of which was to let me know, that Pontiac was at a small distance, coming peaceably, and that he desired me to halt my detachment, until such time as he could see me with his own eyes. His ambassadors had also orders to inform me, that he was Pontiac, the King and Lord of the country I was in.

At first salutation when we met, he demanded my business into his country, and how I happened to dare to enter it without his leave? When I informed him, that it was not with any design against the Indians that I came, but to remove the French out of his country, who had been an obstacle in our way to mutual peace and commerce, and acquainted him with my instructions for that purpose. I, at the same time delivered him some friendly messages, or belts of wampum, which he received but gave me no other answer, than that he stood in the path I travelled in till next morning, giving me a small string of wampum, as much as to say, I must not march further, without his leave. When he departed for the night, he enquired whether I wanted any thing that his country afforded, and he would send his warriors to fetch it. I assured him that any provisions they brought should be paid for; and the next day we were supplied by them with several bags of parched corn, and some other necessaries. At our second meeting he gave me the pipe of peace, and both of us by turns smoked with it; and he assured me he had made peace with me and my detachment; that I might pass through his country unmolested, and relieve the French garrison; and that he would protect me and my party from any assaults that might be offered or intended by the Indians, and as an earnest of his friendship, he sent 100 warriors to protect and assist us in driving 100 fat cattle, which we had brought for the use of the detachment, from Pittsburgh, by the way of Presque Isle. He likewise sent to several of the Indian towns on the north side and west end of Lake Erie, to inform them that I had his consent to enter the country. He attended me constantly after this interview, till I arrived at Detroit, and while I remained in the country, and was the means of preserving the detachment from the fury of the Indians, who had assembled at the mouth of the strait, with an intent to cut us off.

I had several conferences with him, in which he discovered great strength of judgment, and a thirst after knowledge. He endeavored to inform himself of our military order and discipline. He often intimated to me, that he could be content to reign in his country in subordination to the King of Great Britain, and was willing to pay him such annual acknowledgment, as he was able, in furs, and to call him his uncle. He was curious to know our method of manufacturing cloth, iron, &c. and expressed a great desire to see England, and offered me a part of his country if I would conduct him there. He assured me that he was inclined to live peaceably with the English, while they used him as he deserved, and to encourage their settling in his country; but intimated, that if they treated him with neglect, he should shut up the way, and exclude them from it. In short his whole conversation sufficiently indicated, that he was far from considering himself as a conquered prince, and that he expected to be treated with the respect and honor due to a king or emperor, by all who came into his country, or treated with him.

In 1763, this Indian had the art and address to draw a number of tribes into a confederacy, with a design first to reduce the English forts upon the lakes, and then make a peace to his mind, by which he intended to establish himself in his imperial authority; and so wisely were his measures taken, that in fifteen days time, he reduced or took ten of our garrisons, which were all we had in his country, except Detroit, and had he carried this garrison also, nothing was in his way to complete his scheme. Some of the Indians left him, and by his consent made a separate peace; but he would not be actor or personally concerned in it; saying that when he made a peace, it should be such an one as would be useful and honorable to himself, and to the King of Great Britain: but he has not as yet proposed his terms.

In 1763, when I went to throw provisions into the garrison at Detroit,

I sent this Indian a bottle of brandy, by a Frenchman. His counsellors advised him not to taste it, insinuating that it was poisoned, and sent with a design to kill him. But Pontiac, with a nobleness of mind, laughed at their suspicions, saying it was not in my power to kill him, who had so lately saved my life.

In the late war of his, he appointed a commissary, and began to make money, or bills of credit, which he hath since punctually redeemed. His money was the figure of what he wanted to exchange for it, drawn upon bark, and the shape of an otter (his arms) drawn under it. Were proper measures taken, this Indian might be rendered very serviceable to the British trade and settlements in this country—more extensively so, than any one, that hath ever been in alliance with us on the continent.

III) PAGE 37.—At the Council which was held on the 23d of May, 1763, between Pontiac and his Chiefs, and the principal French inhabitants, to induce the latter to join the Indians in their efforts to expel the British, an allusion was made by the Ottawa Chief in his speech, to an incident, connected with the history of Detroit, no other traces of which can now be found. As the speech was delivered in the presence of his own warriors, who must have been actors in the events he described, and to the French inhabitants, who were deeply interested in them, there can be no doubt of the truth of his statement. This war adds another to the calamities, alluded to in the text, which have befallen the town and settlement of Detroit, and it is to be regretted, that its incidents are probably forever lost to us.

"I have no doubt, my brothers," said Pontiac to the French people, "but this war is very troublesome to you and that my warriors, who are continually passing and re-passing through your settlements, frequently kill your cattle, and injure your property. I am sorry for it, and hope you do not think, that I am pleased with this conduct of my young men. And as a proof of my friendship, recollect the war you had seventeen years ago, (1746) and the part I took in it. The northern nations combined together, and came to destroy you. Who defended you? Was it not myself and my young men? The great Chief, Mickinac, (the turtle) said in council that he would carry to his village the head of your chief warrior, and that he would eat his heart and drink his blood. Did I not then join you, and go to his camp and say to him if he wished to kill the French, he must pass over my body, and the bodies of my young men? Did I not take hold of the tomahawk with you, and aid you in fighting your battles with Mickinac, and driving him home to his country? Why do you think I would turn my arms against you? Am I not the same French Pontiac, who assisted you seventeen years ago? I am a Frenchman, and I wish to die a Frenchman."

Pontiac's speech to the French inhabitants upon this occasion, was able and ingenious.

After throwing a war belt into the midst of the Council, he said to the French people, "My brothers! I begin to grow tired of this *bad meat*, which is upon our lands. I begin to see, that this is not your case, for instead of assisting us in our war with the English, you are actually assisting them. I have already told you, and I now tell you again, that when I undertook this war, it was only your interest I sought, and that I knew what I was about. I yet know what I am about. This year they must all perish. The Master of life so orders it. His will is known to us and we must do as he says. And you, my brothers, who know him better than we do, wish to oppose his will! Until now, I have avoided urging you upon this subject, in hopes, that if you could not aid, you would not injure

E

us. I did not wish to ask you to fight with us against the English, and I did not believe you would take part with them. You will say you are not with them. I know it, but your conduct amounts to the same thing. You tell them all we do and say. You carry our counsels and plans to them. Now take your choice You must be entirely French, like ourselves, or entirely English. If you are French, take this belt for yourselves and your young men, and join us. If you are English, we declare war against you"

(IV) PAGE 41.—General Putnam, who then commanded a detachment of Connecticut rangers, accompanied Bradstreet in this expedition. In a letter, which he wrote, dated camp, Sandusky, near the carrying place, Oct. 7, 1764, he reports the speech of Capt. King, one of the Oneida Chiefs, who had been sent with a pacific message by Gen. Bradstreet, probably in the name of the Indians, to Pontiac. This speech was delivered to the warriors of the Six Nations, who had joined the British, and it discloses some points of policy, truly characteristic of Indian negociations

"Friends and brothers—I am now about to acquaint you with facts, too obvious to deny. I have been, since I left you, to Monsieur Pontiac's camp, and waited on him, to see, if he was willing to come in and make peace with our brothers, the English. He asked me what I meant by all that, saying, you have always encouraged me to carry on the war against the English, and said the only reason you did not join me last year, was for want of ammunition; and as soon as you could get ammunition, you would join me. King said there was nothing in it; at which Pontiac produced six belts of wampum, that he had had last year from the Six Nations; he said the English were so exhausted, they could do no more, and that one year's war, well pushed, would drive them into the sea. King then made a stop for some time— Brothers, you know this to be true, and you have always deceived me At which the Six Nations were all angry, and this day they are packing up to go off; and what will be the event, I don't know, nor don't care, for I have no faith in an Indian peace, patched up by presents."

DISCOURSE

DELIVERED BEFORE THE HISTORICAL SOCIETY OF MICHIGAN,

BY HENRY R. SCHOOLCRAFT.

Some Remarks upon the origin and character of the North American Indians. The Iroquois and Algonquins—Amicable relations existing between the Algonquins and the French—The Chippewas, Ottawas and Pottawatamies—Difficulties between the Chippewas and Foxes—Harmony restored between the several tribes—French Supremacy in the Canadas—The Five Nations—Defeat of the Iroquois by the Chippewas—The Iroquois—War between the Chippewas and Sioux—Remarks upon the habits and character of the North American Indians.

DISCOURSE.

Mr. President, and Gentlemen of the Society:

A deep solicitude has been manifested in the history and fortunes of the Indian race. Of the various topics which the discovery of America presented for philosophic discussion, there is none which has so long sustained its interest with the public, or produced conclusions which are more largely the result of gratuitous assumption, or ingenious speculation. Two centuries have but little abated the curiosity with which we regard a people, whose origin is involved in mystery, and whose prominent traits, of features and character, are so widely different from our own. They are identified with the history of our settlement, with the policy of our internal legislation, and with the growth and expansion of our moral and political institutions. American scenery owes to them, one of its most permanent moral associations. Their mythology has peopled our lakes and forests with an invisible creation of super human existences. And their fate and fortune has interwoven throughout our history, many of the most attractive scenes of peril and achievement, which mark its pages. (Note I.)

While the continent itself was supposed to be a groupe of islands contiguous to, or a prolongation of northern Asia, the identity of the population was not doubted. But the moment this error was exploded, and the progress of discovery proved the total separation of the two continents, the attention of the learned was directed to their origin, and the probable time and mode of their migration. On these subjects, ingenuity and research have been exhausted: and the question remains, perhaps, as enigmatical now, as it was at the commencement of the inquiry.

Taking manners and customs, as the tests of comparison, they have been assimilated to various nations of Europe and Asia. But in these comparisons, too great a bearing to certain pre-conceived theories of migration, has impaired the value of the results. Writers have proceeded on the erroneous principle of establishing an identity of race, from such resemblances as could be found, without bringing forward the numerous points of disagreement. The resemblances alone have been employed as proofs, and the dissimilarities overlooked.

It would not, perhaps, be difficult, did the purposes of literary disputation require it, to exhibit *twenty* discrepancies where *one* coincidence has been pointed out. By pursuing the course of proof, which is here reprobated, it would be an easy task, to array as strong a body of facts, indicating a Gælic, a Hindoo, or a Magyar origin, as have ever been adduced to prove their descent from the tribes of Palestine or Tartary. (Note II.)

No great stress should be laid on a resemblance in the mere external manners and customs of barbaric tribes, situated in distant parts of the earth, without a concurrence in language and religion. Similarity of situation and resources may be supposed to lead to striking resemblances in customs, dress, and domestic economy, without necessarily implying affiliation. The fertility of human invention is not so great, but that most men will adopt the same resources, under like circumstances. Place separate tribes of the same stock of men in distant portions of a tropical country, in which cane and bananas are indigenous, and they will continue to subsist on bananas, and cover their lodges with cane. But if one of these tribes migrate to a latitude where the bark of the betula must serve as their shelter, and the northern rice plant supply their food, they will soon reconcile themselves to the substitutes. What dependence, therefore, is to be placed upon the permanency of customs, which are the result of external and accidental causes; which must change with every change of climate, and vary with every mutation of fortune?

Language furnishes a more stable and sure guide, in the comparison of distant branches of the human race. But even here the same tendency is found to employ as a testimony the resemblances only, and to withhold all notice of the discrepancies. To render this means effectual, grammars and vocabularies should be formed both of the indigenous and foreign languages. And when this has been accomplished by a uniform system of alphabetical notation, philologists may hope to contribute their share of intellectual light on the difficult, and for the present, abandoned question of the proximate origin of the Indian race. Even with such materials, great caution will be required to avoid the labyrinth of etymology. The principles of concordance, and of inflection and combination, furnish more certain evidences of remote affiliation, than even sound. Change of accent, which is in slow progress in all languages, will alone constitute a difference in unwritten idioms. But the syntax of a language may be supposed to remain, when the words themselves have undergone considerable, and even complete changes.

A comparison of personal features and peculiar institutions, involving their opinions in medicine and religion, is important. And these topics have been generally employed with less danger from theory and hypothesis. An ancient writer mentions the blue eyes, yellow hair, and identity of form and features of the Germanic tribes, during the first century, as a proof of their being an unmixed and indigenous race. The question is one, rather of physiology than geography. But we may perhaps, with equal reason refer to the prevalence of hazle eyes, black hair and prominent cheek bones, among the North American tribes. Stature is liable to considerable variations from climate. But we do not know that any writer has noticed the slightest characteristic difference in the color of the eyes and hair, and the expansion of the cheek bones, between the tribes situated within the arctic circle, or under the tropics.

History can be applied only to what is known of the Indian tribes, within a comparatively recent era. Oral tradition is important as an auxiliary species of information; but it is nearly useless when unsupported by written or monumental history. From the tendency of the Indian tribes to exalt themselves in prowess and original consequence, and to supply the lapses of history by stretches of the imagination, a continual caution is required in recording traditionary information; and a constant reference to cotemporary authorities, both oral and printed. All unwritten tradition, extending beyond the era of Columbus, may be considered as entitled to little credit. It is not in the nature of their institutions to preserve the memory of events beyond a few generations. And were they more prone to exercise their intellectual faculties, the rigour of their situation has, at all times, absorbed their principal care. Without letters, without syllabic signs, and with only a partial use of hieroglyphics, there never could have been much reliance upon their ancient traditions. Their monuments, if they can in strictness be said to have any, are equally unsatisfactory. They generally indicate a people in the rudest state of society, who made stone clumsily answer the various purposes of iron, and buried their dead above ground, probably for the simple want of a shovel to dig a grave. They piled one body upon another, for reasons obvious in erratic nations, and they chose high places of burial, to be out of the reach of the periodical floods. This we consider the most reasonable explanation of the mounds which have been referred to, as evidences of their skill in geometry, of their idolatry, populousness;—and in short, of any thing, but what they appear, in reality, to have been, rude barrows of the dead!

The accumulation of facts and materials on all, and each of the points which serve to illustrate their history and character, is an object of enlightened research. And it is a species of research which recommends itself particularly to our attention,—situated as we are, in the vicinity of numerous, and some of them populous tribes, who preserve the living languages, and the traditions, customs and institutions of their ancestors. Other societies are favorably located to preserve the materials of our national history. It is our province to glean upon the frontiers.

As yet, no attempt at a general history of the North American Indians, has been made. There are some accounts of particular tribes, several tracts on their languages, occasional papers, reports, and other materials, either in the evanescent form of pamphlets, or scattered through a variety of publications—all of which, it would be important to collect and preserve. By consulting the best informed chiefs, and some of our elder inhabitants, interesting facts might be gleaned from local tradition, and from unpublished letters and manuscripts. All that relates to the languages, is still within our grasp. But every season is narrowing the circle from which the information is to be drawn. Much of what is most desirable to be known, has already perished with the prominent actors who have appeared on the scene. Much, however, still remains. To rescue, both what is written, and what is unwritten, is an appropriate and laudable object of literary research.

In calling your attention to one of the principal Indian stocks, whose wars and migrations are identified with the history of the Upper Lakes, and the extreme North Western portions of the Union, it may be proper to advert, for a few moments, to the great era, in which our acquaintance with the race of red men commenced. Whether we refer to that era to acquire a correct knowledge of their former condition and character, or to trace the early events of their mournful history, it must ever be a subject of regret, that the first voyagers to America had not evinced, either more care in observing, or more discrimination in recording the interesting facts before them.

The age of the discovery, fruitful as it was in daring enterprise, was not characterised by severe scrutiny or deep research. Still less was it marked by liberal and exalted sentiments in politics, philosophy or religion. Columbus himself suffered his better reason to be swayed by the splendid fallacies of visionaries, such as Mandeville and Marco Polo. And he narrowly escaped the charge of heresy for advancing some of the modern doctrines in geography and astronomy. Monarchs held, that the accident of discovery gave them a right, not only to the sovereignty of the new world, but also over the personal liberty of the natives, who were wrested from their homes to be exhibited as spectacles in the courts of Europe, or sold as slaves in their markets. And learned and pious men gravely deliberated whether the new found people were to be treated as brethren of the same species.

The spirit of maritime adventure was, however, at its height. Sovereigns vied with each other in the glory of discovery, and the thirst for foreign dominion. Portugal, and the cities and little republics of Italy, took the lead in the splendid career of adventure. And at the same time that they set the example to the rest of Europe, they furnished them with experienced nautical commanders. Unfortunately too, they set the example of enslaving the native inhabitants of the countries they discovered, and of causing every nobler aspiration to give way to the thirst for wealth, and the rage for political aggrandisement. The natives of both the East and West Indies, after their strange looks and dress had been scanned, and their stranger languages listened to, were, in reality, regarded in scarcely any other light than as furnishing the ready means of accumulating " barbaric pearl and gold."

All that related to their intellectual character, internal polity, political divisions and subdivisions, distinctive languages, and the agreement or disagreement of their traditions, respecting their origin and dispersion over the two continents was looked upon, either as matter of minor importance, or left to the chance of future observation. In perusing the collections of these early voyages, it is surprising to see in how purely a mercantile spirit they were executed; the dry minuteness with which unimportant incidents are described; and the great paucity of exact, comprehensive or discriminating views. And it can therefore create but little disappointment, if the inquirer into this portion of our aboriginal history, should often be a gleaner in a barren field.

Cabot is admitted to have been the disoverer of the Atlantic coast of North America from Newfoundland to the latitude of the capes of Virginia, or possibly, the Carolinas. (1497.) He was followed, twenty seven years later, by Verrizani, who, making the land in about the latitude of the present capital of Georgia, ran along the coast to the 56th degree of north latitude. Neither of these discoverers made extensive observations upon the coast, or the native inhabitants. They landed in but few places, and of those few, there is scarcely one, that, from their descriptions, can be certainly identified. It has been conjectured that Verrizani entered the straits between the highlands of Neversink and Long Island, where he had an interview with the natives. And if so, he preceded Hudson, in his discovery, eighty-three years.

In the interim between the dates of these two voyages, the Portuguese navigator, Cortereal, visited some of the higher latitudes of the North Atlantic; and discovered and named the coast of Labrador. (1500.)

About this epoch fishing vessels began to resort to the Grand Banks, giving rise to a branch of commerce in which the French and Portuguese appear to have first taken the most active part. Jean Denis, a native of Rouen, who had sailed on one of these fishing voyages, (1506) is said to have laid down and published the first chart of the coast. Two years afterwards Thomas Aubert, another of these private adventurers, brought the first natives from Newfoundland to Paris; and claimed to have made certain discoveries on the gulf and river, since named St. Lawrence, which have been generally deemed apocryphal. As little credit has been awarded by historians to the reported visit of Velasco, and the etymological proofs of the Spanish origin of the word "Canada."

It remained for Cartier, sailing under commission from Francis I. to discover and name the St. Lawrence, which he ascended in one of his ships, to lake St. Peters, and his boats, to the rapids above Montreal. And from this period (1535) the chain of northwestern discovery remains unbroken and undisputed. (Note II) The French were not slow in availing themselves of the advantages the country presented for settlement. But their first efforts were unsuccessful, and they encountered the most determined opposition from the Iroquois, or Five Nations, whom it was the fate of Cartier to have offended, by ascending the river against their declared will, and by carrying off one of their principal chiefs, who died in France. To dissuade him from ascending the river above the island of Orleans, they made him profuse presents of maize and fish. One of the Chiefs then drew a circle in the sand, and waving the multitude to retire, took Cartier and his followers within it He then commenced speaking, and at separate intervals, presented him three children, two males and one female, to divert him from his object. The multitude, at each presentation, setting up a loud shout. Finding him still resolute, they then resorted to the influence of a conjurer, who, after certain ceremonies, announced to the French, that the Indian God had uttered his maledictions against them; and that there was so much ice and snow in the country, that whoever entered it, must die. They opposed the discovery by every means in their power: and when the French had got a footing, they omitted nothing to dispossess them. With more than Carthagenian hatred they resisted the progress of their growth and settlement, nor did they cease to resist, while the French had a fortress to defend.

To oppose this confederacy the French courted the alliance of the Algonquins; a nation, who, in the time of Champlain, were settled along the north banks of the St. Lawrence between Quebec and lake St. Peters, extending north, by the Utawas, to lake Nepising. Their power and influence were however spread, by the ties of affinity, among a very extensive circle of tribes, towards the north and west. (Note IV) From the head of lake Erie, they advanced under various names, along both banks of the great chain of communication through the lakes, extending north to lake Winnipic and Hudson's bay, and south, to the mouth of the Ohio. They were also connected by ties, less closely drawn, but not less indicative of a common origin, with the principal tribes of New England, and of the mountainous passes east of the St. Lawrence. The latter were collectively called Abenakis, or Eastlanders. (Note V.)

Aided by allies thus widely dispersed, and favorably situated, the French prosecuted the war against the Iroquois. The latter were supported by the English, and by such Indian auxiliaries as they could command. And this continued to be the state of affairs, till both the English and French outgrew their dependance upon Indian power. To this general state of alliance there were two notable exceptions, consisting of interchanges of hostility between affiliated tribes, which exposed each of them to the resentment of their parent stock. The Wyandots or Hurons, who are not only of the Iroquois type of languages, but are placed by the French at the head of that family, joined the French. The Foxes who, on the contrary, speak a well characterised dialect of the Algonquin, adhered generally to the Iroquois. (Note VI) And this unnatural alliance had nearly proved the extermination of both these tribes. The Iroquois pursued the Hurons with the inveteracy of a family quarrel, and drove them from the St. Lawrence to the banks of the lake, which has since taken their name. A band of them were settled, through the piety of Father Marquette, at Michilimackinac. Others fled into lake Superior, and even took shelter, for a time, in the country west of it.

The Foxes, by attempting to keep terms with both parties,

pleased neither. They soon drew upon themselves the enmity of their kindred tribes, and the execrations of the French, who heaped upon them, and their vascillating policy every term of reproach. They were driven from old Toronto, through the straits of Niagara, to Detroit, where they played a conspicuous part in the Pontiac war. (Note VII) They afterwards concentrated their remaining force at Green Bay; where they formed a close alliance with the Sauks, and, for a time, sustained themselves. But they were pursued by the French, with the aid of the Chippewas and Menomonees. They were beaten in two sanguinary battles on the St. Croix and Fox rives—fled to the Wisconsin, and finally sought refuge west of the Mississippi.

The accounts which some writers have given of the ancient and firm alliance between the Iroquois and Algonquins, it is too late now to investigate, either for the purpose of disproving, or corroborating. The state of pupilage in which the Iroquois are represented as having been placed, without authority to hunt, or to exercise the usual privileges of savage freedom, is not, however, rendered probable by any thing we know of this warlike people, since the discovery. And the whole relation savors much of one of those ingenious fictions, by which one rude nation endeavours to acquire credit for exalted sentiments, at the expense of another. That these rival nations, were at some remote period, on terms of amity, is not improbable; but if such amity was the result (as it seems) of the fear of overgrown power on the one side, it was in most imminent danger of being interrupted, the moment an increase of numbers, brought the weaker in a condition to cope with the stronger power. From whatever causes the disagreement arose, it is certain the league had been broken long before Roberval displayed the French flag upon the St. Lawrence, or Van Twiller hoisted that of the United Provinces upon the Hudson. And the successful ambuscade and decisive battle, in which the Iroquois were defeated by the Algonquins on the river Beckancourt in Lower Canada, shows that the war was prosecuted with a spirit of enterprise and determination, which owed no part of its efficacy, to either French or English counsels.

It is due to the French character, in relation to these two celebrated tribes, to remark that they *found*, but did not *make* them enemies. They turned the contest to their advantage, by forming a league with the party from whom they had most to hope, and most to fear. And the league thus early formed they never broke. They attended the Algonquins in their hunting parties and their war parties; in their days of feasting and of fasting; in their councils and their battles. They followed them through every rigor of the country and the climate. They formed settlements in their remotest villages, and cemented their friendship by intermarriage. With but little change of expression they seemed to have adopted the protestation of the Moabites; "Whither thou goest, I will go. And where thou lodgest I will lodge. Thy people shall be my people. And my God, shall be thy God."

It was among the tribes and kindred of this nation that the French exercised that high power and influence, which has rendered their colonial history so celebrated. By gaining this ascendency they succeeded—after a long and bloody contest, (in which the city of Montreal was once taken by storm and sacked,)—in repelling the attacks of the Iroquois, and curbing their power. They drew a line of forts from the St. Lawrence to the Gulf of Mexico, and thus matured that daring plan for annihilating the British power in America, which was once the cause of well grounded alarm. But the final blow to French power was not given by the Iroquois tomahawk and scalping knife.

it was the long and valorously sustained effort of the fleets, and armies of the illustrious nation, and the hardy colonists, from whom we are descended.

In ceding the jurisdiction of the country, the French population did not, (like the Spanish in Louisiana at a later period,) withdraw from it. They remained in their settlements, and were tolerated in the enjoyment of their civil and religious privileges. With a numerous population, the government of France also left behind, the reputation of great enterprise in extending its authority, great bravery in defending its territorial rights, and unwearied devotion in reclaiming the Indian tribes. They carefully explored the geographical features of the country, and seized with much judgment upon the most commanding positions for forts and trading houses. They carried the fur trade from Gaspe bay, where it may be said emphatically to have been commenced by Cartier in 1534, to the banks of the Saskatchawine. If they did not improve the system of agriculture practiced in France, at the several eras of colonization, they at least, kept pace with it. (Note VIII.) We are indebted to them for some of the choicest natural fruit of Normandy and Brittany. In their intercourse with the Indian tribes they were kind and conciliating. A better exemplification of the paternal character of their government and the impression it has left upon the northern tribes, cannot be given, than by quoting some passages of a speech delivered by a Chippewa Chief in 1826. "When the French arrived at these Falls, they came and kissed us. They called us children, and we found them Fathers. We lived like brethren in the same lodge, and we always had wherewithal to clothe us. They never mocked our ceremonies, and they never molested the places of our dead. Seven generations of men have passed away, but we have

not forgotten it. Just—very just were they towards us."
And their eventful history will long remain conspicuous for
the ardor of their discoverers, the devotion of their missionaries, and the heroic valor of their commanders. (Note IX)

When their commerce began to extend itself to the Upper
Lakes, they found seated around the borders of these
internal seas, the Three Brother Tribes—the Chippewas,
Ottawas, and Pottawatamies. These tribes appear to have
been originally, a single scion of the Algonquin stock.
Their own traditions affirm, that they came from the east,
and reached lake Huron together. Their separation into
distinct tribes, took place in the vicinity of Michilimackinac,
(Note X.) where the Ottawas, who were most inclined to
agriculture, remained. The Pottawatamies pushed their
fortunes southerly through lake Michigan, and after several
mutations, both of name and place, finally established themselves about its head. The Chippewas, whom it is my
intention more particularly to notice, extended themselves
northwardly, through the straits of St. Mary, to Lake
Superior, and westwardly, from that lake to the Mississippi,
where they first came in contact with the Sioux. At what
period this migration took place; how long a time it occupied; and what were the particular incidents attending it,
their traditions have failed to inform us. The French found
them, where they now are, around the shores of lake
Superior, and north and west of it. As they first encountered this tribe in fixed habitations at the Sault of Ste Marie,
they gave them the appellation of *Saulteurs*. They migrated
by the southern shores of the lake, and kept their warriors in
advance. This advanced party, who at a subsequent
period acquired, and have retained the name of Mukundwa,
or plunderers, proceeded west to the Mississippi, and established themselves around the rice lakes at its sources.
Tradition is silent, also, as to the name and condition of the

people whom they encountered on lake Superior. At Lapointe, near the west end of the lake, they were surprised to fall in with their own relations, the Ottagamies or Foxes who had reached that place by an overland route, from Green Bay.

These two tribes lived on terms of mutual friendship for a time, the Chippewas occupying the lake border, and the Foxes living on the small rice lakes at the sources of the Ouisconsin and Ontonagon. Their hunting parties first came into collision. Disputes arose, which were exasperated by recrimination, and a general war preceded by some personal conflicts ensued. The French threw their weight into the scale against the Foxes, and having mustered a strong force of Indian auxiliaries, totally defeated them in a general action at the junction of the Wolf and Fox rivers. The strenuous efforts they made to exterminate this tribe, have been paliated on the plea of its insidious and treacherous character.

The Chippewas of the Lake also prepared to inflict a decisive blow. War messengers were despatched along the whole line of the lake coast from Lapointe to St Mary's. Four hundred volunteers, from the different villages, obeyed this invitation. They assembled and united in the ceremonies of the war dance, on the open shore of the lake.— They were headed by Waub Ojeeg, or the White Fisher, a bold and successful warrior, who had commanded in six previous expeditions, and acquired the respect and confidence of the surrounding bands.

While the mental discipline, by which a party of warriors, is wrought up and prepared for war, is strongly calculated to excite reflection; their departure from the sacred fire, around which they have sung their songs, recited their former exploits, and pledged their vows, cannot be contemplated, without mingled feelings of pity and admiration. No rolling of drums, no sounding of trumpets, no unfurling of ensigns, is there. They quit the scene with gestures of defiance, but at the same time, with a fixedness of purpose and spirit of heroic daring, beyond all that is known to the civilized soldier. When the yell of final onset is raised, there is a quick interchange of passionate sensations between the actor and the hearer, of which the ancient sound of defiance of the shield and javelin may furnish a coincidence, though not a parallel. Tradition has preserved another incident of the departure of this expedition. When the warriors filed through the village to enter the forest, they were met by the collected matrons of the place carrying their infants in their arms, and uttering that wail, in the shrill tenor voice of the Indian female, which bespeaks affliction, and which whoever has heard, will not soon forget. Such an appeal was unusual. The whole party stopped. One of the elder men then came forward, and addressed them in a short speech, in which he reminded them of the relative duties of warriors and women. They then proceeded, following a westerly course.

After this party reached the waters of the river St. Croix, they encamped six nights, on their downward passage, before they discovered signs of the enemy. They proceeded with great caution, keeping scouts in advance. On the seventh day the scouts discovered the Foxes encamped on a portage. But they came so suddenly upon them, that they could not give the alarm. Both parties fired at the same moment, and a general action commenced. The Chippewas came up with great promptitude. They formed along the line of the portage path, hemming the Foxes in a peninsula formed by a bend in the river. The action was long contested, but terminated in the total defeat of the enemy, very few of whom escaped. Many were drowned in attempting to cross the stream, being precipitated over the falls. Among the slain were found several of the Sioux, who aided the Foxes on this occasion.

This action took place at the great falls of the river St. Croix. It put an end to the feud between the Chippewas and the Foxes. The latter abandoned their villages at the rice lakes and retired down the Ouisconsin. The sequel of their story may be told in a few words. After a separation of more than half a century, these two tribes again met, but under widely altered circumstances. Time had effected a great revolution of feeling on the part of the Foxes. They had recovered their shattered fortunes, and in part, recruited their population, by an intimate union with the Saucs, and with the small tribe of Iowas. But they had lost nothing of their warlike character and reckless spirit of adventure. They were engaged in fierce hostilities against the Sioux, their ancient allies, and were thus by the force of circumstances but without any purposed concert, brought into a state of political alliance with the Chippewas.

The meeting took place at Prairie du Chein in the summer of 1825, and was attended with more than ordinarily imposing circumstances. (Note XI.) The Foxes, Sauks and Iowas were here to meet, not only their allies the Chippewas, but their open enemies the Sioux. They came to discuss the subject of a settlement of boundaries, willing to listen to terms of accommodation, but prepared for war. They ascended the channel of the Mississippi in a flotilla of canoes, so arranged that they moved up the stream in a compact body. Not a woman nor a child was with them. It was exclusively a party of armed warriors, painted and decorated in the most gorgeous manner, singing their war songs and beating their drums, with their barbaric ensigns displayed. In this attitude of warlike array, turning a point of land, they presented themselves in sight of the village, the whole male population of which, together with the assembled tribes of Indians present, rushed to the banks of the river, to witness the advance of this novel spectacle. As the flotilla approached, it became apparent that the music and shouts were accompanied with dancing. The canoes were attached together, upon which a platform was erected. They passed slowly up against the strong current of the river, keeping the Island shore, until they reached a position opposite the Sioux encampment at the upper part of the village, where their shouts and dancing became more than usually animated. They then wheeled slowly into the cr——d, keeping up their animated cries, and descended along the line of the village to an open place below. To this point the throng of white and red men had followed, anxious to witness the debarkation of men thus flushed by their recent successes, and vain of their exploits. Kokue, their war captain, led the way. Pointing with his lance to the crowd on shore, he motioned them to make way, to admit his landing. The crowd obeyed. He instantly leapt ashore and was followed by his whole party. They marched directly into the plain, and halted in line. They then stacked their spears and rifles, and stood within grasp of them. All this was effected with the precision and alacrity of drilled troops. In the mean time the Chippewas had arranged themselves, in an irregular line, in front. After a short pause, some of their aged chiefs advanced into the open space. This was a moment of intense and painful interest. But it was soon relieved. They were met by the Fox Chiefs, with a friendly salutation, and taken by the hand. Nor has any thing since occurred to interrupt the harmony between these tribes.

In reverting to the early period of these intestine feuds, between brethren of the same genealogy, we are carried back to a very interesting era of our Indian and Colonial history, when the French still maintained their supremacy in the Canadas. The English settlements had not yet expanded beyond the sources of the streams, flowing into the Atlantic. They rested, in New-York, on the Mohawk—in Pennsylvania, on the Juniata, and in Virginia, in the valley of the Shenandoah. The summits of the Alleghany had not yet been crossed. Oswego and Niagara, Le Boeuf and Du Quesne still bore the Gallic flag. The names of the Ohio and the Wabash, the Mississippi and Missouri—and still more emphatically, those of Huron and Michigan, were listened to, as so many words calling up the idea of a distant wilderness of vast, but indefinite extent; bearing, in its geographical features, a giant outline, and filled with large and fierce quadrupeds, and savage tribes, whose very names were a source of terror.

The place in which we are now assembled, was among the number of these remote and solitary points, in the vast panorama of western woods and waters. It owed its early celebrity to its connexion with Indian affairs. It then contained a feeble population, clustered around a military post, and living, rather upon the industry of the natives, than upon their own. If they possessed some immunities in their seclusion, they were those of the aspirant under the sword of Dyonysius. They depended upon a thread. Surrounded by fierce and predatory tribes, they were agitated by the breath of every war party, who set out with vows of vengeance, and returned with shouts of victory. Happy would it have been, if these errant parties had returned with only the exultation of honorable warfare. But the pinioned prisoner, and the bloody scalp, filled up the melancholy spectacle. That venerable receptacle of Indian trophies, the Government Council House, where the price of blood was so often paid, perished in the conflagration of 1805— and with it, it may be hoped, a policy, which in its whole scope and tendency, deserves to be mentioned, only in terms of the deepest reprobation. Other countries had set the example of binding victims on the rack, and burning martyrs at the stake. It remained for the representatives of Christian sovereigns, warring in the woods of America, to stimulate savage barbarity, by setting a price upon the heads of women and children, who were roused from their slumbers by the war whoop, and struck down by the war club. Nor is it undeserving of notice, that the weapons used in these murderous assaults, were solemnly dedicated to the work of plunder and massacre, by being passed, in public council, through the hands of the local commandant, that he might exclaim in the symbolical language of the Indian, "We take hold of the same tomahawk."

It is enough to advert to this dark era, to awaken reflections of deep and painful interest. But there is no pleasure in dwelling upon its sanguinary incidents. It is consolatory to reflect that when history and tradition have gleaned whatever can be recovered of those early times, the half of the tale of horrors will not be told. They are only referred to, as constituting an era, in which the Indian population was strong, and the European weak. When they held vast possessions, and we little. When, in fine, the whole line of our inland frontier, from the Savannah to the Penobscot, quailed beneath the menaces of Indian power. Among the tribes, who struggled for supremacy, the Five Nations held the most conspicuous rank. They had not yet felt the pressure of causes, which were destined soon to arrest their course, and to leave them, like the tribes against whom they contended, feeble and dependant. They roved at will, from lake Champlain to the Illinois. They had imposed tribute upon the Mohegans, who inhabited the mouth of the Hudson, before the discovery. This tribute was paid yearly in shell-fish. They had humbled the Delawares, and placed them in a state in which they could neither make treaties, nor sell lands, without their consent. They exterminated the Eries. And they defended and brought off the Tuscaroras, and adopted them into their confederacy. They extended their war parties south, to the mouth of the Ohio. And they claimed, and actually sold the lands to the banks of Kentucky river.

They were not satisfied with carrying their conquests towards the south and west. They pushed their war parties north to lake Huron, by the route of lake Simcoe and Nadowasaking, where they found and subdued the mixed tribe of the Mississagies. They passed through this lake to the island of St. Joseph, in the river St. Mary, where a severe action took place, betweeen them and the Hurons. This action was fought on the water, and in canoes. They were not deterred by the partial discomfiture attending it. They passed deeper into the northern regions, and exhibited themselves, in a strong body, on the borders of lake Superior, at a prominent point, which perpetuates their name and their defeat.

Point Iroquois, or (as it is called by the Indians) the place of Iroquois bones,* is at least 900 miles from the general seat of the Iroquois Council fire at Onondaga. At this distant spot, in the career of their conquests, flushed with victory, and confident of success, they encamped. It is said a prisoner was sacrificed to stimulate the thirst of vengeance, and to swell the number of melancholy, but in general, doubtful instances, in which man has voluntarily polluted his lips with the flesh of man. But in the height of this infernal ceremony, retribution was at hand. Their passage through the river, and the audacious and reckless spirit which they had every where manifested, had been narrowly watched. The Chippewas hastily mustered their forces, and prepared to follow them. When they had

*Nadowàweguning

reached the head of the straits, opposite the Iroquois camp, the weather became threatening; and it was debated whether they should not defer their passage till the next day. In this dilemma their prophet or seer was appealed to, and he, after the usual ceremonies, declared a favorable omen. They awaited the approach of night, and embarked in two divisions. The darkness of the night was extremely favorable to their enterprise. The parties landed at separate places, and formed a junction in the woods, in the rear of the Iroquois camp. The prophet here declared another favorable omen. They then sent forward some scouts to observe the condition of the enemy, who appeared totally unconscious of danger, and were still singing their war songs. It was determined to remain in their concealed position, till the enemy had gone to sleep. It then commenced raining. They advanced in the rain and darkness, cautiously feeling their way to the edge of the woods. They then made the onset. The struggle was fierce, but of short duration. As had been concerted, each lodge was surrounded at the same moment, the poles lifted, and the tent precipitated upon the sleepers, who were despatched as they started up, bewildered and entangled in their tents. A great slaughter ensued. Very few of the Iroquois escaped to carry the news of the disaster; nor did this nation ever renew their inroad.

About the same time, (1680) some of the other northern tribes made a successful effort to repay the injuries, they had received from the Five Nations. A party of 400 Iroquois having, in one of their western excursions, reached the banks of the Maumee river, surprised the camp of the Miamis and Illinois, killed upwards of 30, and took 300 prisoners among whom were a great proportion of women and children; with this trophy they commenced their return, confident in their strength, and the dread their name had inspired among the western tribes. The discomfited Miamis prepared to avenge their loss. They obtained the aid of some of the tribes in alliance with them, and made a hasty pursuit, keeping far enough in the rear to avoid premature discovery, and determined to improve the first opportunity to concert a stratagem. Fortune came to their aid. A rain storm commenced, and continued with such violence, that they were confident the Iroquois would stop. The rain fell incessantly from morning till evening. Conceiving this a favorable opportunity, they pushed on with such diligence, that they got in advance of the enemy. They concealed themselves on the sides of the trail in meadow grounds, where the grass screened them, and the make of the ground afforded a favorable position for attack. When the Iroquois had entered the defile, the Miamis started up, and pouring in from all sides, threw them into confusion. The panic of the Five Nations was further increased, on discovering that the rain had rendered their fire-arms useless, and they were compelled to rely chiefly on their war clubs. In this contest the superior activity of the western Indians, in the management of their native weapons, became manifest. One hundred and eighty of the Iroquois fell, the rest retreated fighting, till night put a stop to the conflict. The Miamis recovered all their prisoners, and effected a safe retreat.

A very different result, however, generally attended the Iroquois expeditions towards the west and north.—Their track was literally marked in blood. But it was blood doomed to be atoned for, by future humiliation.—Their career has terminated as inauspiciously, as if they had never sacked villages, and exterminated tribes. No foresight could have anticipated that the lapse of time would bring back this proud and conquering people into the upper lakes, as supplicants to the north western tribes for a small tract of ground to raise their corn upon, and to serve as a refuge for their children. Yet such are the facts exhibited by the treaty of purchase made by the Iroquois delegates of the Menominees and Winebagoes in 1821. This treaty took place at Green Bay, near which the Iroquois settlements have been gradually accumulating. Six years later, at Butte des Morts, they formally smoked the pipe of peace with the northern Algonquins, after a war, which, without any formal cessation, is known to have continued the better part of two centuries. (Note XII.)

In looking to the causes which gave the Iroquois such a preponderance over the other tribes, the advantages of a close union, and their local position at the sources of so many important streams, have been mentioned by their eloquent historian.* But it is quite evident that the great and efficient cause of their success existed, in their having early acquired the use of fire arms, while the western tribes adhered with obstinacy to the bow and club. Even after the lake tribes had obtained a supply of fusils, they still hankered after their ancient arms. And twice, within half a century (from 1762 to 1812) they formed confederacies against the whites, based on a total renunciation of the use European manufacture. (Note XIII.)

But little can be said in corroboration of the opinion which has been advanced, that the Iroquois were a superior race of men, to other of our tribes: and in support of which, their valor and exploits, and particularly their skill as diplomatists and orators, have been adduced. Brave they undoubtedly were, according to the Indian idea of bravery. As far as mere brute force could triumph, they triumphed. But with all their achievements, they never acquired the moral courage to spare the vanquished after battle. They never elevated themselves above the savage principle, which does not distinguish between a public and a private foe. They

*Clinton.

did not separate, in their border wars, the idea of renown acquired in open battle, from that of secret murder. The scalp, torn away with stealthy footsteps at midnight, was as honorable a trophy as that taken on the contested field in open day. In what, therefore, were they distinguished above the other tribes? Among the cruel, they were the most cruel. Among the treacherous, the most treacherous. It is true they were gifted with a bold and enterprising spirit. They were skilful to plan, and quick to execute. They suffered with astonishing fortitude the pains they expected to inflict upon others. When taken in battle they asked nothing, and they expected nothing. The whole history of martyrdom may be challeged for a parallel to the almost superhuman courage and constancy exhibited by the Iroquois captain put to the torture at Fort Frontenac, as described by Charlevoix. In him the glory of triumph had apparently extinguished all sense of physical suffering. But apart from this species of heroic endurance, their traditional history is relieved by few instances of highmindedness, or mental abstraction. Still less do we find those instances of clemency which throw a charm over history. They could bear, but not forbear. The strong traits of savage character were mingled, as in other instances, with savage virtues or savage magnanimity. But they were perpetually veering between the extremes of human passion. For one Logan, or Garangula, they produced an hundred inferior orators. For one friendly Gyantwa,* twenty sanguinary Brandts.

Republicans themselves, and a confederacy of republics, they fought against the only two nations, of modern times, who have exhibited plans of governmental improvement—the French and the Americans. And they only became our friends, at that point, when they could no longer re-

*Cornplanter.

main our enemies. For their aid, as friends, we can perhaps point to Fort Stanwix and the Niagara frontier. For their ire, as enemies, we can point, and history will forever point, to Oriskany and Cherry Valley, Wyoming and Schoharie. In our own times, they have produced a Skenandoah and an Owyawatta,* (better known as Red Jacket) the one an eminent example of the triumph of social and christian principles—the other, as noted for his inveterate adhearnce to the maxims of savage life. Many of them have nominally professed christianity, and renounced paganism. But under very favorable circumstances for acquiring knowledge, and practising the arts, they have made but few permanent acquisitions. Their population has dwindled away in a state of profound peace, on the best corn and wheat lands in America. Learning, in the select youth, has produced despondency. Ardent spirits, has relaxed their courage and constancy, and annihilated their enterprise. Danger, the strong bond of their union, by being withdrawn, has left their confederacy to fall into harmless fragments, and exhibited them, like the fictitious hero of a modern tale of genius:

"Link'd with one virtue, and a thousand crimes."

The war between the Chippewas and Sioux forms a conspicuous figure in the history of the northern tribes. But it has been a war of detail, conducted by separate Chiefs and bands, without general concert, and without producing, at any one period, general calamity. There have been no great battles—no formidable expeditions—no bloody ambuscades. Petty skirmishes, sudden inroads, affrays of hunting parties, the surprise of a few lodges, or personal rencontres, make up its common incidents. Occasionally, something more formidable has been attempted, but in general, their large parties have effected but little, one party or the other, frequently *both*, giving way after the first onset. It is the

* Saggoyawatta.

policy of Indian warfare to operate by surprise. Parties are hastily mustered, strike the blow, return and disperse, before their opponents have time to rally. This produces retaliation. Surprise is repaid by surprise. Robbery by robbery. Murder by murder. And when no other cause disposes the parties for hostilities, a vow, made during sickness, the loss of a friend, a dream, or the desire of personal distinction, supplies new actors on the scene.

A hundred years of this species of warfare, between the Chippewas and Sioux, interspersed with seasons of partial and insecure peace, has rendered the hatred between them hereditary. No one knows certainly when the war commenced, how it originated, and what have been its principal incidents. Tradition is not agreed on these points In some accounts, it places the origin in 1726. Generally, it attributes it to disputes respecting hunting grounds. Sometimes to the deceitful policy of the Sauks and Foxes. Sometimes to domestic incidents of a romantic character. All these causes have probably operated, and each exasperated the effects of the other. In modern times, peace has often been concluded, and as often broken. Temporary causes have led to these hasty arrangements, but no hearty reconciliation appears ever to have taken place. The peace-pipe has scarcely been smoked on one part of the lines, before the war club has been raised on another. The treaties they have made under the auspices of our government, have been assented to, more to show their friendship for us, than for one another. One cause of the difficulty of effecting a firm peace, is probably to be found in the great extent of their frontier, being upwards of five hundred miles on the line of the Mississippi. Each band has some separate quarrel or interest. Each chief claims for himself and his followers the highest powers of sovereignty, taking up and laying down arms, whenever convenient, without submitting the question to a general council of the nation. This is the radical defect of Indian government.

In a war carried on in this loose and desultory manner, nothing else could be expected, but that the lives and fortunes of the white men, whom accident placed in their power, should become the sport of whim and caprice. A few years ago, Cheanacquot, a noted war leader from the Leech Lake sources of the Mississippi, conducted a small war-party against the Sioux. When they had reached the vicinity of Dickson's Trading House, he determined to direct his attack against that post. The party approached the house with great circumspection, creeping among the grass, till they came within a few hundred yards of the enclosure. They here concealed themselves behind a fallen tree. While thus hid, Mrs. Dickson and her eldest daughter approached from another part of the scene, and stopped in earnest conversation within reach of their guns. It was a moment in which life and death were at stake. The warriors cocked their pieces. Revenge and clemency struggled for a moment in the breast of Cheanacquot. He wavered—beckoned to his party not to fire and springing from his concealment, offered Mrs. Dickson his hand. Transported with this act of magnanimity, where magnanimity had not been looked for, she invited the chief and his followers into the house, where they were regaled and dismissed with presents.

A different result attended the expedition of Kewanocquot. This chief, during the summer of 1824, mustered a party of twenty-eight men from the Chippewa villages, at the sources of the Ouisconsin and Ontonagon. They embarked in canoes on the river Saulteur, which they descended to the junction with the Mississippi. They concealed themselves behind an eminence which commanded a wide prospect of the Mississippi and the shores of lake Pepin.

No enemy could, however, be discovered. They remained in this position two days, and began to give up the hope of achieving any thing. Towards the evening of the second day, a canoe of white men was descried ascending the Mississippi. It was the ill-fated Finlay, an inhabitant of Prairie du Chien, with three canoe men on his way to St. Peters. He encamped at the foot of lake Pepin, pitched his tent and planted his flag in front of it. All this was seen by the Indians from their places of concealment. Kewanocquot and his followers visited the tent for the purpose of gaining some knowledge of the Sioux. They were received with the customary civilities, presented with some tobacco, and departed. Not, however, before they had witnessed striking evidences of fear, on the part of the canoe men. This was a fatal weakness.

When the party had got some distance from the tent, one of the warriors in the rear, said—"When I go out hunting I do not like to return without killing something." "Nor I," replied several voices around him. An immediate rush took place towards the tent, and several shots were fired in quick succession. The details of this massacre may be easily imagined. The three canoe men were killed on the beach. Finlay, although wounded, attempted to escape by plunging in the water, and for a time evaded the shots fired at him. But he too, was fated to die. All the bodies were then scalped, and the tent plundered.

Of this scene Kewanocquot, with twenty of his followers, remained a silent spectator, sitting in his canoe—a leader without decision, and without authority. At last he said to the murderers,—"Why do you so! Had they not given us tobacco and vermillion?" Fear immediately fell upon the whole party. They cut their canoes, turned them adrift, and proceeded home by land. (Note XIV.)

About this time the slumbering war between the Chippewas and Sioux, broke out with fresh vigor, on the borders west of the Mississippi. A strong party of Chippewas were treacherously fired upon, while peaceably encamped under the walls of Fort Snelling, and under the protection of its flag. Four persons were killed and eight wounded. The assailants then fled. But they were demanded by the proper authorities, and an equal number of Sioux given up, to satisfy the justice of the Indian law. These men were accepted by the Chippewas, by whom they were shot down as they walked, without apprising them of their fate. It was hoped the affair would here drop. But there is no point at which the Indian law of retaliation stops, short of the extermination of one of the parties.

The following year a small party of Chippewas were seized at Lac Qui Parle, while returning from a visit to the post of St. Peters, and six persons put to death. Reparation was demanded for the injury; but the messengers were treacherously killed. The Chippewas prepared to avenge the loss, and sent out a numerous war party, who returned however without finding the enemy.

Time will not permit me to add further details of a war, as hopeless in its termination, as it is inglorious in its results. Of the general state of the contest, it may be observed, that the advantage has generally been with the Chippewas, whenever the parties have encountered each other in the woods. The reverse has happened in contests in the *prairies*:—the peculiar skill and expertness of local habit producing these differences. The Chippewas appear to have been first led into the Mississippi Valley, in pursuit of the larger animals, whose flesh is used as food. They are undoubtedly conquerors of the territory they possess in that quarter. But the conquests must have been made at an early day, as they appear to have been terminated prior to the arrival of the French. The border population on both sides has long been stationary. Whatever advantages the northern bands have possessed, as being better woodsmen, and perhaps earlier habituated to the use of the fusil, the density of the Sioux population has proved a counterpoise. The struggle would long have remained doubtful, had not the Sioux found a new, and most formidable enemy on their southern border, in the modern confederacy of the Sacs, Foxes and Iowas.

These numerically small bands, after having been nearly annihilated in previous wars, appear to have been resuscitated in the genial plains of the Mississippi. By acting in close union, and adopting the use of the rifle; keeping a public magazine of powder; and making their inroads on horseback—for which the nature of the country is favorable, they have within a short period wrested from the Sioux a large extent of territory. And they bid fair, in martial exploits to become the Iroquois of the Mississippi. Hemmed in between these tribes on the south, the Chippewas on the north, and with no powerful allies on the line of the Missouri to flee to, the Sioux bands are in danger of being still further curtailed of their territory. The natural effect must be, a diminution of the supply of animal food, and a declension of numbers.

But not they only,—our entire Indian population appears fated to decline: not so much, it is apprehended, from the want of external sympathy, as from their falling under the operation of a general principle, which spares neither white nor red man, but inevitably dooms all, who will not labor, to suffering and want. Accustomed to live on game, they cannot resolutely make up their minds to turn agriculturists, or shepherds, or mechanics. They have outlived the true hunter state of the country, yet adhere, with a fatal pertinacity, to the maxims of a wandering life. They pursue their intestine feuds with as determined a rancor, as if they still had ample stores of animal food, and unbounded ranges of territory to flee to. They cannot be persuaded that there is any better mode of living than that pursued by their forefathers; or any species of freedom superior to the state of savage independence. This is the whole mystery of their decline; however, other secondary causes may have hastened, and may still continue to accelerate it.

They have been taught, from early life, that tilling the earth is dishonorable. That war is the true path of glory. That happiness consists in sensual enjoyments. That forecast is distrust of providence. The acquisiton of property degrading, and generosity the test of greatness. But their generosity often degenerates into extravagance, and their trust in providence into an excuse for indolence. Their aversion to labor is often to be traced to the fear of ridicule. Their contempt of wealth, to the rage for popularity. The desire of personal distinction is frequently indulged at the expense of private rights, and of national faith. Bravery is often another term for assassination. And riot a milder word for homicide.

These remarks may appear severe, but they are not intended to be so. They are conceived to be just, and we may appeal for their truth to every person of observation who has been long and intimately acquainted with our Indian tribes. No one can be insensible to the heroic traits of the Indian character. To his open hospitality—his constancy in professed friendships—his filial piety—his resignation under suffering, his valor in battle, and his triumph at the stake. No nation, perhaps, ever felt a stronger love of country, or cherished a deeper veneration for their dead. And they linger round the places of their sepulture as if conscious that the period of separation was limited, and the soul itself immortal.

There is a charm cast over the hunter's life, which it is

easier to appreciate than describe. There is something noble in the situation and circumstances of the Indian, who confident in his own skill, is buoyed up in his frail canoe, or trusting to his own prowess, plunges into the deepest forests, reckless alike of want and danger—roving at will, without the ties of property to embarrass, or the obligation of laws to restrain him. But it is the charm of poetry, and not of real life. It is sweet to the contemplation, but bitter to the taste. The pleasure arises from associations, which few will stop to analyze, but every heart can feel. It is a pleasure which will remain, and be cherished as a species of intellectual talisman, long after the people, who are the sources of it, shall have submitted to their probable fate.

To withhold them from that fate, is an object of high and disinterested attainment,—difficult to be accomplished, if we may judge from the results of all experience. But it is a labor in which we cannot err on the side of clemency and magnanimity. In which treasure may be lost, but reputation must be acquired. Our character as a social and intellectual people, has often been judged, and we may say prejudged, by our treatment of the Indians. Their condition has been referred to, in terms coupled with charges of delinquency in the great duties which a civilized owes to an uncivilized people. Remiss we may have been in some things; and in others, fallen short of the jealous expectations of philanthrophy and religion. It was difficult, in every exigency, to reconcile the duties of self preservation, with simultaneous efforts of improvement. But the difficulties were no sooner removed, than the efforts were renewed. And there is no period of our history, as a separate nation, in which their welfare and preservation has not entered largely into our internal policy. (Note XV.) But in order to perceive how inadequate either the giving or withholding of extraneous aid has been, to produce some of the principal evils of their present condition, it is only necessary to advert to a few general facts.

In adjusting the ratio of population to the means of subsistence, it has been estimated that eight acres of ground will support an agriculturalist. But it may be doubted whether the range of 8,000 acres will support a hunter. Assuming this quantity, however, to be adequate, it would require a territory equal in extent to the state of Illinois, to subsist a tribe of 5,000 souls. And it may be doubted whether the whole area of North America, east of the Mississippi, was adequate, considered as the separate hunting ground, of the various tribes, to subsist the estimated Indian population at the era of the discovery. However this may be, little doubt exists that the native population was over-rated at that era. And it has been over-rated at every subsequent period. No one, who is conversant with the facts, but knows that it is over-rated now. It had reached its maximum before the settlement of Jamestown, or Plymouth; and it has declined under every varying aspect, since. But in a ratio so fluctuating and irregular, as to admit of no comparison with the rise or fall of any other people.

The use of European luxuries, and the contention of European armies, with whom they have usually allied themselves, has doubtless very injuriously affected particular tribes. But their general declension may be sought in causes more constant in their operation, or more widely spread and destructive in their effects. Disease has swept away more than the sword or the bottle. Ignorance of the rationale of medical treatment has exasperated their simplest maladies. Internal dissentions; scanty and unwholsome food; the effects of alternate abstinence and repletion; violent transitions from heat to cold—from intense and sudden exertion, to listless indolence; contempt of regimen a reliance on mystical medicines and superstitious rites, have alternately acted as cause and effect in reducing their numbers, and exasperating their condition. If we look closer to the constitution of the Indian mind, and their domestic habits,—to their proverbial indolence and improvidence; their blind devotion to a dark and wild belief in sorcery and magic, and the paralysing effects of the doctrine of fatalism, we shall see other causes of their abasement. And many of these causes are totally independent of the proximity of a white population. (Note XVI.)

But it is not to be concealed, that there exist causes of depression, which date their origin with our institutions. Nor to be denied that they present strong claims, both on our justice and our sympathy. The whole body of the Indian nations, east of the Mississippi, present themselves in the attitude of dependent tribes—looking up to us for measures, and sentiments and feelings becoming a prosperous and high minded people. No research is necessary to inform us that they were once numerous, and are now feeble. That they once occupied a vast territory which is now ours. That they were once rulers, where they are now subjects. Enough is before us to mark the great stages of their political mutations, and to show, by an appeal to the past, what may be anticipated for the future. All will be ready to concede, that their prospective fortune is gloomy. Not, because it does not promise to reinstate them in political power—for the sooner that was destroyed, the better for their own sakes—but because, after the experience and exertions of two centuries, there is, in reality, so little ground to hope for their speedy convertion and civilization; because they have evinced, and continue to evince, so little aptitude for the useful arts, and are so slow in perceiving, and acknowledging, the superiority of the agricultural over the hunter state. Because they cling with such obstinacy to those habits and opinions, rites and maxims which constitute the strong features of the Indian character. (Note XVII.)

They neither desire our knowledge, nor our religion. They are not in a situation to appreciate our customs or institutions. They distrust our power, decry our refinements, and condemn our laborious industry. All the motives that can operate on unenlightened minds—pride of character, the hope of fame, the fear of evil, tend powerfully to oppose civilization and christianity. The Jew is not more wedded to his peculiarities, nor the Mussulman to his slothful habits, and erroneous faith. (Note XVIII.)

We have no desire, however, by dwelling on the difficulties inherent in the task, to discourage renewed efforts. Far less to cast them off from our sympathies. As a people, we still owe them a great moral debt, which begins to press more and more upon us, and will press heavier and heavier upon our children. This debt it was not for our ancestors, who incurred it, to cancel. They had other and paramount duties to perform. Driven from the intolerance of the old world, they threw themselves upon the untried dangers of the new. They did first what was of the most imperious necessity. And they left to us, to accomplish the unfinished labors and acquisitions of a new people. They left us to extend the benefits of moral and religious instructions, till they should embrace the remotest territory, and the humblest inhabitant. To aspire high in political wisdom, mechanical ingenuity, and nautical achievement. To excel in the exact and natural sciences, and to form and fashion a vernacular literature. Last, not least, in the bequest of national duties, they left us the native tribes to provide for; to strive by timely aids to smooth their passage through this life, and to prepare their minds for the realities of another. Let us fulfil the expectations of justice and humanity. But let us fulfil them with the understanding, as well as with the heart; neither leaving this people to struggle unaided against the evils of their situation, nor running the hazard, by attempting violent and sudden changes in their society and institutions, of plunging them still deeper in misfortunes. A noble but persecuted race, are sending up their appeal. They have drank freely of the bitter cup of affliction. They are every year becoming fewer in numbers; more impoverished in means, more degraded in character. Let us allay the malady, we cannot cure. Let us forgive the errors we cannot approve. Let us not despair of accomplishing, what man can accomplish, nor doubt in those things which are the province of God.

NOTES.

(1) Page 53 INDIAN HISTORY.—It is remarked in the London Quarterly, that the Indians of North America are, to the learned of this continent, what "the fallen arch, the broken column, and the incrusted medal" are to the philosophers of Europe. But we may be permitted to add, that the history of the former, is enveloped in a more impenetrable mystery. To render the parallel exact, it will be necessary to admit, that the base of the arch is obliterated, the column is shattered into fragments, and the medal is without date or inscription. The study of our Indian history is, indeed, to a great extent, the province of the antiquarian, rather than the historian. Few, however, have attempted either branch of the inquiry, without discovering the paucity of the materials, both written and monumental, to be examined.

While this degree of uncertainty rests upon their origin, the time and mode of their migration to the continent, and their ultimate division into numerous tribes, we have it in our power to secure much valuable data respecting their present condition, and numbers, and the location of the principal interior tribes. We live in an era favorable to missionary and school efforts, and which is particularly characterised by the temperance enterprise. It may be safely said, that there is a degree of interest awakened for the improvement of the condition of the western Indians, which has marked no other era since the discovery. This interest is concentrated, and may be judged of, by reference to the transactions of missionary and education societies. But while the cause of Christianity is thus advocated, and the claims of the Indians brought forward, there is an appropriate sphere of duty for literary societies, who may prove useful auxiliaries, by fostering a liberal spirit of inquiry, and by exciting renewed interest in their history, languages, or existing institutions. Piety and literature may thus go hand in hand, in promoting the cause of Indian civilization. Under this view, the prospectus and plan of a society of Inquiry respecting the Indians, was adopted by a number of benevolent individuals at Detroit in 1832, under the title of the Algic Society. Some of its proceedings have been made public. Its first anniversary was held at Detroit on the 14th of October, 1833. By a vigorous prosecution of the object, it is conceived that the cause of philanthrophy may be subserved, and renewed interest awakened in the condition and prospects of a noble, but persecuted race.

The following account of the Chippewa and Ottawa population in lakes Huron, Michigan and Superior, and in the upper Mississippi north of St. Anthony's falls, was reported, at the anniversary meeting of this Society. It excludes, however, the entire Pottawattomie and Menomonie population, and also the villages of Ottawas south of Grand river, and river Au Sauble.

	Men.	Women.	Children.	Metifs.	Aggregate
St. Mary's river	58	73	144	161	436
Lake Superior	197	258	475	123	1006
Upper Mississippi	369	493	851	122	1855
Rainy lake	118	125	201	32	476
Red river & Red lake	226	224	388	336	1174
River St. Croix	233	254	328	80	895
Chippewa river	369	397	567	106	1376
H'ds of Wisconsin &c.	84	92	153	13	342
Bay d' Noc of Green bay	45	52	98	15	210
Lake Huron N. shore } Michilimackinac	31	47	73	147	302
Straits of Michigan	46	54	120	14	274
Peninsula of Michigan north of Grand river	1350	1566	2384	374	5,674
	3144	3571	5752	1553	14,020

(II) Page 54. HUNGARIAN, OR MAGYAR LANGUAGE.—This language is alone, and remote from every other. The notices which philologists give of it, are very interesting. It appears to have slight analogies with the Finnish, Laplandish, and Esthonian—also with the Chadesh, Teutonic and Slavonian, but its roots are original, and cannot be traced to any hitherto discovered source.

As in the Indian dialects, extensive use is made of suffixes, by which nouns, verbs, pronouns and prepositions are modified. Conjugations are seldom made by auxiliary words, but by particles post added to roots.

    Ir   he writes   Ojib.   Ozhibeiga.   he inks it
    Ir-at   he causes to be written
    Ir-at-at   he can cause to be written
    Ir-at-at-am I have been able to cause to be written.

There are two classes of *vowels*—masculine and feminine. In consequence, two classes of conjugations run through the language.

Pronouns are either cut in two, when used with verbs &c. and the verb &c. inserted between the two halves, as

Mienk (our) atya (father) becomes miatyank, our father.

Or, more commonly, they become postfixes, by adding their terminals to nouns, as

Noun.
{ Haz   house   Ojib. Wakiégon.
  Hazam   my house
  Hazad   thy house
  Haza   his house
  Hazunk   our house
  Hazatok your house (plu.)
  Hazok   their house

Verb.	Varok	to wait		
	Varoz	I wait	Ojib.	Ninbi
	Var	thou waitest		
	Varunk	he waits		
	Vartok	we wait		
	Varnak	ye wait		
Preposition	Bennem	in me	Ojib.	Peenjini
	Benned	in thee		
	Benne	in him		
	Bennunk	in us		
	Bennetok	in you		
	Bennek	in them		

Sok (many) added to nouns for plural number, in time became abbreviated into ek, ak, &c as ember (man) emberek (men) lab (foot) labak (feet.) This termination is not used when a noun of number precedes. Ket ref (two ell,) not ket refek (two ells.) Sok ezer virag (many thousand flower,) not viragak (flowers.) Ezy sereg Katona (a troop of soldier) not katonak (soldiers.)

The particles asz and esz, attach personal service to the object, as hal (fish) halasz (fisherman.) Kert (garden,) kertesz (gardener.)

Ka and ke are diminutives
Sag and seg imply office or rank.

Apat	abbot
Apatsag	abbacy
Puspok	Bishop
Puspokseg	Bishopric.

At or et, convert the root (or third person of present tense) into substantives

Gondat	he thinks	Ojib.	Inaindum.
Gondalat	thought		
Felel	he answers	"	Nuh ko dum.
Felelet	an answer		

The same rule applies to the conjugation of verbs and the declension of nouns, and the prepositional changes

There are scarely any laws of syntax. Marton gives 16 different arrangements of the sentence, my father has sold his house. The following is one of them

az	atyam	a	haz	at	eladta
Indefinite article	Father—with mas. poss. pronoun fr enyim (mine) om	definite article	House — at, instead of a, for the sake of euphony		Adta—from add the root of adni to give, whence aladni to sell.

The translation of this sentence into the Ojibwa, is as follows:

Nos	Oji	Odawa	Owakiegon
My father, from neen (my) and os (father)	He did—(past tense, third per. indic. mood)	Sell (third per. sing to sell)	His house, (not his tent, wigwam) nor his home (aindaud) but a house (or fort) of English construction.

This arrangement may be altered, by placing the noun objective before the other members of the sentence.

While, it will be observed, in this hasty outline, that there is a total difference in the sounds of the language, it presents nevertheless, some coincidences and resemblances to the Indian dialects of this continent, in grammatical principles, which may render it interesting hereafter, to refer to it.

(III) Page 16. ERA OF TRADE IN VIRGINIA.—The English were slow, in taking part, in the settlement of colonies. Forty nine years, after Cartier's first visit, viz. in 1534, Sir Walter Raleigh sent out his first ships to Virginia. They were under the command of Amadas and Barlowe, who landed on the coast and traded with Granganimo, the brother of the king. A tin dish was exchanged for 20 skins rated at 20 crowns, and a copper kettle for 50 skins, worth 50 crowns.—*Hakluyt's Voyages.*

(IV) Page 62. KENISTENO TRIBE.—This tribe is included in the circle, and forms its most advanced body in the northwest. They speak a well characterized dialect of the the Algonquin. Their name is derived from the al verb *kenisa*, to kill. Mackenzie remarks that they came from the east, and that the track of their migration has been undeviatingly northwest. In 1775 Frobisher found them at the Missinipi (great water) or English river—a tributary of lake Winnipec. And this was the extent of their progress north. They drove back the previous occupants, whom they despised and held in contempt on many accounts, especially for their ignorance in hunting beaver and stretching and drying the skins. In derision they stretched and hung up the skin of a frog, to taunt their enemies, on the *Portage de Trait*. Who the people were, whom they expelled, is not known. It was not the Chippewyans.

(V) PAGE 62. GREAT FAMILY OR STOCK OF THE ALGONQUIN, OR ALGIC TRIBES.—Wide as this circle is represented in the text, and numerous as are the tribes included within it, there is reason to believe, from the strong analogies of language and customs, supported by the general tradition of an ultimately south or south western origin, that they were but branches of still more powerful affiliated tribes who in the course of their migrations, occupied the whole Atlantic coast from the Carolinas to the Gulph of St. Lawrence. There is reason to believe that the course of their migrations was in general northeastwardly, crossing in their track, the Potomac, Susquehanna, Delaware, Hudson, Connecticut, Merrimack and Penobscot, until they reached the confines of the gulph and river St. Lawrence, by which they were turned northwestwardly, until some of the tribes reached the remote points on the northwestern frontier, where the Algonguin population now rests. That portion of this stock, put off branches westwardly, who in time, came again into juxtaposition with the original line, after they had acquired distinctive peculiarities of language &c. is rendered probable, by all that is known of their earlier history. And this process of intermingling, after long separations, became more intricate, as time and distance, were added to their migratory career. Yet their is enough left, in the strong resemblances of a common language and common traditions, manners and customs, to afford proof which is almost demonstrative, that this extensive portion of North America, was peopled by a single original nation. We are not strenuous of their generic appellation. Call them Algonquin (or for brevity's sake, *Algic,*) Lenapi, Penthusian, or Ostic, it maters little, if the allusion be broad enough to cover the whole geographical area of their former and present residence. We see strong resemblances in language between the Shawnee (formerly residents of the Carolinas,) and (what Mr. Jefferson denominates) the Powhattan language, and still stronger coincidences, in sound and syntax, between the latter and the modern Ojibwa. Equally striking is the parallel between the latter and the Mohegan as recorded by Edwards, and scarcely less so, between the Algonquin and the Narraghansett and the Pokanoket as given by Roger Williams. These affinities assume a stronger type, when we come to compare by the Algic standard, the modern dialects of the Cree or Kenisteno, Muskigo, Mississagee, Ottawa, Pottowattomie, the current Menomonee, the Fox, Kickapoo, Miami, &c.

The theory of a numerous class of original languages on this continent, and in Europe and Asia, which we see supported by M Balbi, may comport with the pride of philological discovery in Europe. But so far as relates to the North American tribes, we believe the radical stocks to be few. Not over *three*, or *four*, have been satisfactorily made out, between the gulph of Mexico and Baffin's Bay, although the dialects are numerous, and the chain of migration somewhat complicated. But when we take from this area the anomalous languages east of the Mississippi, namely the Iroquois, the Wyandot and the Winnebago, there is removed, from the field of inquiry, much of the difficulty of classification. Indeed, we are decidedly of the opinion, that all that remains, within these geographical limits, are susceptible of being traced to Floridic, or Algic roots.

(VI) PAGE 62. FOX OR MISKWAKI LANGUAGE.— A characteristic difference of this language, is, the substitution of l, in words wherein the Chippewas use n.

(VII) PAGE 63 PONTIAC WAR —The following facts are mentioned in the British annual Register for 1763.

"On Lake Erie, with a crowd of canoes, they (the Indians) attacked a schooner, which conveyed provisions to the fort of Detroit, but they were not so successful. Though in their savage navy they had employed near 400 men, and had but a single vessel to engage, they were repulsed, after an hot engagement, with considerable loss. This vessel, was to them, as a fortification on the water, and they could not make their attacks with so much advantage as upon the enemy by land."

Subsequent numbers of the same work state—That on the 3d of April, 1764, Sir William Johnson concluded, at Johnson Hall, on the Mohawk, preliminary articles of peace and friendship with 8 deputies of the Seneca nation, which was the only one of the Iroquois, who had joined Pontiac.

In August 1764, General Bradstreet granted "Terms of Peace" to certain deputies of the Delawares, Huron and Shawnee tribes, at Presque Isle, (Penn,) being then on his way to relieve Detroit. By this treaty, they agreed to deliver up all the English prisoners.

In October of the same year Col. Bouquet, granted similar terms to an other deputation of Shawnees, Delawares, and other tribes who had been active in the war, at Tuscarawas, (now in Ohio.)

The delivery of the English prisoners was subsequently made by the western Indians, and gave rise to the exibition of a feeling of attachment to these prisoners, which is in striking contrast to their usual cruelty in war.

Most of these prisoners had been adopted as children, or received as members of Indian families. "From every inquiry that has been made "adds the Editor," it appears that no woman thus saved, is preserved for base purposes, or need fear the violation of her honor No child is otherwise treated by the persons adopting it, than the children of their own body The perpetual slavery of those captivated in war, is a notion which their barbarity has not yet suggested to them. Every captive whom their affection, their caprice or whatever else leads them to save, is soon incorporated with them, and fares alike with themselves."

(VIII) PAGE 65 Mackenzie observes that the French had carried agricultural implements and wheel carriages to Fort Bourbon on the banks of the Saskatchawine long before the conquest of Canada.

(IX) PAGE 66. The following was received from an Indian Chief at the treaty of Buttes des Morts in 1827 twenty nine years after the date of it It has been retained, as illustrative of the policy with which the French received the requests of the Indians; and also of the care of the latter in preserving writings to which they attach value.

"St Louis, le 15 Avril, 1798.
Les Sauvages porteurs sont des Ottawa folavoines et Potawatamia qui vont en guerre sur les Chicaichas et qui me demandent le present pour se faire connoitre aux blancs a qui ils se présenteront, et à qui nous les recommandons.
                                         JENON TRUDEAUX"

(X) Page 66 MICHILIMACKINAC.—This place has been the capital of the north west fur trade, and Indian exchange from an early period. Many interesting data might be embodied respecting it. We have only leisure to advert to a few The present settlement on the Island, dates in 1764 The year previous the British garrison, on the peninsula, was massacred by a combined movement of the Ottawas and Chippawas Troops were sent up, the following summer under the command of St Clair, who negociated with the Indians for the Island, and built the Government House, at that place. He remained in command until 1782, in which year he was relieved by Capt Robinson. The fort was surrendered to the American Government in 1796. It was taken by the British in 1812, resisted an attack from a detachment of the American army and navy in 1814, and was surrendered, on the mutual restoration of conquests by the terms of the treaty of Ghent Its Indian history, is deeply interesting, involving, as as it does, the incidents of an extensive frontier.

(XI) PAGE 69. TREATY OF PRARIE DU CHIEN OF 1825.—A treaty was concluded and signed at this place by the various tribes of Indians on the 19th of August, and copies of it delivered to each of the parties, accompanied by the usual ceremonies which are necessary to solemnity to this act in the eyes of the Indians. A broad belt of wampum on which the United States government and each of the nations present were symbolically represented, and the union established between them, was passed through the hands of each chief and warrior, thereby signifying their individual assent to the treaty; and this belt was afterwards deposited with the commissioners. Several strands of wampum were attached to each copy of the treaty delivered to the different tribes, with the intention, I pre-same, of having this document transmitted and explained to each of the principal persons in the nation. The pipe of peace was reciprocally smoked, after which the ashes were carefully knocked out, and the pipes themselves presented to the Commissioners.

Were these ceremonies intended for any effect they might be calculated to produce on the minds of the bystanders, they might certainly be regarded as exhibitions of serious trifling, or ridiculous solemnity. But whoever has had occasion to reflect upon the character of the North American Indians, must be aware of the great importance which they attach to these ceremonies and the weight which is given to our transactions with them, when a decent respect is paid to their ancient customs, and national forms. In their eyes the lighting up of a council fire, the smoking of a pipe, or the delivery of a strand of wampum, have all the importance of opening a debate, settling the preliminaries of a peace, or delivering a sealed instrument into the hands of a national express.

By this treaty a peace has been concluded between the Chippewas and Sioux, and between the confederated Sauks, Foxes, Iowas, and Sioux. Thus the principal nations who have so long maintained an inveterate war with each other have terminated their hostilities. To perpetuate this peace the above-named tribes have established boundaries between their respective territories, and agreed to confine their hunting excursions within their respective limits, unless the permission of the adjoining tribe, to hunt upon their lands is previously obtained. It is believed that this course, hitherto unattempted, will take away the fruitful source of these wars, which are generally to be traced to the effects, either immediate or remote, of a dispute respecting boundaries. It is believed also, that the peace which has thus been concluded in a full council of the tribes, by ample deputations of the first chiefs and head men, and after mature discussion, will be kept in good faith.

The treaty also includes, in its provisions, the Winnebagoes, Menomonies, and Pottowatomies, with the Chippewas and Ottawas of the Illinois, respectable delegations of whom, were present, assisted in the discussions, and signed the treaty. The peace heretofore existing between these tribes, has been renewed, and boundaries established between their lands. A great and good work has thus been commenced, highly honorable to the character of the administration under which it has been planned and executed, and highly auspicious to the future condition and prospects of the Indians. Further exertions will, however, be required to perfect this benevolent plan, to watch the fulfilment of treaty stipulations, to perfect and extend the lines where the work has been left unfinished, and to embrace other tribes, and the remote bands of the contracting tribes, within its scope.

It is creditable to the character of the tribes respectively, that during the whole time of their attendance at the treaty, they conducted themselves with soberness and propriety, exhibiting much of that austerity of manners, which has been often remarked both in remote and modern times, as a characteristic trait of our Indians. An observer less busied than myself in other duties, might have found much to admire and to record in scanning the costume, the dances and attitudes, and the distinctive national traits of the several tribes.

The Indians evinced an accurate knowledge of the geography of the country, and no mean share of acuteness in supporting their claims to territory, by reference to their early history, the location of their villages, and the usual routes of their hunting parties and war parties. These recitals were illustrated by maps delineated upon birch bark, or parchment, a mode of illustration in which the Chippewas, the Sauks and Foxes appeared to be particularly expert. Where claims were set up to vast portions of the same country by each contiguous tribe, on various pretences, among which was the novel right of *recent* conquest strongly urged by two of the tribes, and where there were such conflicting interests, feelings and opinions, fortified by the predjudices of ages, it may be readily conceived that much scope was afforded for discussion, and considerable opportunity given for that peculiar specie of intrigue and manœuvering, which is known to appertain to an Indian treaty.

(XII) PAGE 76 TREATY OF BUTTES DES MORTS —The following boundary line was agreed upon, at this treaty, between the Chippewas and Menomonies.

Beginning at the Plover portage of the Wisconsin, (where it was left at the treaty of Prairie du Chien of 1825,) running thence, in a north eastern course, to a point on Wolf river, equidistant from Oshawano and Post Lakes of said river, thence to the falls of Pashaytig river of Green Bay, thence to the forks, or junction of the Meesaukootag or Burntwood river with the Menomonie, thence to the Big Island of the Shöskmaubic, Smooth Rock river, thence following the channel of said river to Green Bay, which it strikes between the *Little* and *Great* Bay de Noquet

(XIII) Page 76 CAUSES OF INDIAN HOSTILITY —One of the latent causes of Indian hostility, are mentioned in a familiar letter of General Washington, addressed to Col Humphries in 1791 After allusion to the existing war with the western Indians, then being prosecuted by General Wayne, he adds this gloomy prediction, "though I must at the same time, confess, I cannot see much prospect of living in tranquility with them (the Indians) so long as a spirit of land jobbing prevails And our frontier settlers entertain the opinion that there is not the same crime (or indeed no crime at all) in killing an Indian, as in killing a white person "

(XIV) Page 81 AFFIDAVIT, AND LIST OF THE NAMES OF THE WAR PARTY OF KEWANOCQUOT —"The subscriber, a trader among the Indians at the post of L'Ance, on the south shore of lake Superior, whence he had just arrived express, testifies to the following occurrence.

A war party of Chippewas went out from the south shores of lake Superior, early in the present season, to find the Sioux. The whole party consisted of about thirty warriors, headed by Kewanocquot of *Vieu Desert* On the Mississippi river, they fell in with an American trader, with a small party of men in a boat, who were armed, and carried the national flag. The Indians went to them—entered into conversation—received tobacco, and departed

During the evening they returned, seized and disarmed the party, and killed and scalped four persons, including the trader, or person in command They then took the flag—plundered the boat and fled, carrying with them the scalps. These scalps have been danced through various parts of the country between lake Superior and Green Bay, after the Indian manner, and thus the war cry raised. The trader, a person in charge of the boat, when first assailed, asked for mercy—said that their enemies, the Sioux were encamped near, and that if they spared his life, he would conduct them to the spot. But his appeal was disregarded.

This affair took place so near to Fort Snelling at the falls of St. Anthony, that the morning gun could be heard. Such is in brief, the relation of the Indians at L'Ance, where the scalp of the principal was received. From an inspection of the scalp, it appears to have been taken from a middle aged man. The hair is light brown mixed with grey.

Signed in duplicate,
JOHN HOLIDAY.

"Taken and subscribed at the office of Indian Agency at Sault de Ste. Marie, this thirty first day of August 1824, before me
HENRY R. SCHOOLCRAFT,
*U. S. Indian Agent, and Justice of the Peace
for the County of Michilimackinac, M. T.*"

Mr. Holiday brought the scalp referred to, in a small black coffin, which was transmitted to the Governor of the territory. A surrender of the murderers was demanded, with threats to take them by force, if this demand was not complied with. In consequence eighteen warriors of the party, with the chief, surrendered themselves at the Indian office at St. Mary's, in June of the following year. On examination, seven of them, were committed to the jail of Mackinac, to await their trial for murder. During the winter of 1826, after a confinement of several months, they used their knives in cutting an aperture through the timber of their apartment, and escaped to their villages in the vicinity of Lac du Flambeau.

The following is a list of the names of all the men who composed the war party, with their places of residence. The asterisk indicates those persons who participated in the murders.

No.	Name.	Translation	Place of residence.
1	Kewanocquot (chief)	The returning cloud	Vieu Desert, head of Wisconsin.
*2	Sagito	He who makes afraid	do
3	Nizhoda	Twin	do
4	Waswagun	The torch	do
5	Kaychiosh	The fast sailer	do
6	Pasigwitung	The one who gets up	do
*7	Cacabisha	The screech owl	do
8	Ogabeianacwut wabi	He who sits on the last cloud	Ontonagon
9	Padamikonce	The little singed beaver	do
10	Madwaywa	Noise	a roving character
11	Gitchi Mitakoossiga	Great pure tobacco smoker	Trout Lake
12	Matawkoossigans	Little pure tobacco smoker	do
13	Bawdask	He who sails hither	do
*14	Wamitigoshence	The little Frenchman	do
*15	Ockwaygon	The Neck	do
16	Waygimanwiguon	The Chief Feather	do
17	Antoine Gardron	(a half breed)	do
18	Mamajigwun	The moving Feather	do
19	Moas o gitick	Moos's knee	do
20	Kawabindiba	The white head	do
*21	Kazini	Shaved head	Wabachitamon lake
*22	Naiwajiwunos	The central Rapid	do
*23	Annimikence	The little Thunder	Lac du Flambeau
24	Wawbun	The day light	do
25	Nitawawchi	The dexterous dodger	do
26	Kaybayosa	Last of the Hunters	do
27	Chawonigizluck	South Sky	do
*28	Otagami	The Fox Indian	do

(XV) Page 85 NATIONAL POLICY RESPECTING THE INDIAN TRIBES —Legislation on Indian affairs, is peculiar to our government. At least, if any of the European powers, who possess colonies in America, have made the condition and improvement of the native tribes the subject of legislative enactments, we are not apprised of it. There are no statute books handed down from other generations to guide the legislator in his course, by pointing out modes of policy approved by success, or condemned by failure. It is a branch of internal policy, not only peculiar to our legislative history, but peculiar to modern times. It has grown up by imperceptible degrees, as the advance of society, the world over, has favored humane, liberal and enlightened sentiments—as the absence of predatory wars has permitted our government to turn its attention to plans of improvement, and as the justice and equity of the claims of the Indians themselves have been considered and allowed.

The British Parliament seldom or never dignified the subject by entering it on their journals. No Sharp or Wilberforce appeared to advocate the claims of this suffering portion of the human family. No Burke or Chatham electrified Senates by eloquence in their behalf. Under the sway of the mother government it was exclusively the subject of executive decision, and those officers entrusted with the administration of affairs, settled the necessary questions upon the spot, or recommended measures for adoption at court. It was not deemed necessary to strengthen the executive arm by parliamentary enactments. Moneys were voted for colonial purposes in the supply bill, under such general heads of appropriation as left the subject—always one of minor importance, free for the exercise of executive discretion.

The sovereignty of the Indian territories being admitted to lie in the crown, the abstract right of the natives to the soil, if it was recognized at all opposed no obstacle to government purposes. The local authorities took what land was wanted, and gave the Indians such equivalents as were judged proper. They also accepted their services in war, and listened to their complaints in peace. Agents were stationed at suitable points clothed with the king's authority, and the relation of a father to his children was thus kept up between the executive and his Indian subjects. A relation altogether conformable to Indian notions of political power, and with which, there is reason to believe they were well satisfied. The French, had practised the same system before them, adding the wrong-headed project of christianizing without simultaneous attempts to civilize them, as a part of it. And intimately blending the ecclesiastic, military, commercial and executive policy; or rather, placing all in strict subservience to the latter. If there was any thing wrong in theory, they made abundant amends for it, in practice.

To this system, in declaring a separation from the parent state, we succeeded. Some of the same officers who had participated in its duties, under the British government continued to exercise similar functions under the confederacy. Others, and by far the greater number, with Sir John Johnson at their head, adhered to the royal cause, and by the predatory system they adopted, very much embittered a strife, that, of itself, stood in need of no extra stimulants. Time has thrown its softening tints over these sanguinary deeds, and we should severely reprobate any attempt to revive the feelings under which they took place. They were the errors of nations, contending for what each believed to be its most sacred rights, and like the errors of individuals, we think that party ever exhibits the greatest proofs of an ennobling spirit and an enlarged philanthropy by whom they are soonest forgiven and forgotten.

"Ah need I paint the deeds that dyed with gore
Wild Raisen's waters, or Wyoming's shore,
Or lift the misty veil of mellowing time,
That hides Lucinda's fate, and Carleton's crime."

During the provisionary government of the revolutionary contest, the subject of Indian affairs, was managed by a committee of Congress, who decided the necessary points referred from the frontiers, and performed the executive as well as legislative duties appertaining to the subject. They acted chiefly by resolution. They recommended to the Indians to remain neuter, and to pursue their ordinary occupations. They imported goods on the credit of Congress, to supply their most pressing wants, provided rules to be observed by those who went to trade in the Indian country, and replaced agents at the proper points, to see these rules enforced, and keep the government properly advised of the true state of affairs. These agents were, among other duties, empowered to license traders, to designate the places at which trade should be conducted and to exercise a general superintendence over the conduct of both traders and Indians—points of government police, which it has been deemed necessary to continue under various modifications, to the present times. The journal of this committee affords the germs of several subsequent laws, giving ample evidence of the care and foresight which they bestowed upon the subject.

These provisionary rules appear to have governed the practice of the Indian Department, for several years after the adoption of the constitution. And we find but few enactments of Congress on the subject during the entire presidency of Washington, a proof that the executive power had been exercised in the most satisfactory manner. Under his administration agents were appointed to reside at important points on the frontiers, and a system of surveillance and correspondence organized, which centred in the War office, as the most suitable channel of approach to the executive. Congress, however, being the absorbent of all powers not particularly delegated, began slowly to resume its interest in Indian affairs, and thereby to define or limit the executive power. And as the progress of this resumption or appropriation of power exhibits a history of our legislation on the subject we shall briefly advert to it.

The first act, under the constitution, to regulate trade and intercourse with the Indian tribes, was passed during the administration of Washington, (1790,) limited in its duration to two years. This act was continued, for limited periods, in 1793, '96, '99—and until experience proved the necessity of a permanent law. In 1800 Congress authorised the executive to cause issues of provisions to be made to Indians visiting the military posts and agencies—to direct the payment of expenses attending the visits of chiefs and deputations to the seat of government, including necessary presents to them; and also requiring separate abstracts of the provisions issued to be kept at the war department.

It was, however, reserved for Mr. Jefferson, who brought into the presidential chair a personal knowledge of Indian character, and entertained the most humane and liberal sentiments towards them, to introduce what has been deemed the organic law, on the subject of Indian affairs generally. This act, which was passed in 1802, embodies all that was probably worth retaining of the previous laws on Indian trade and intercourse, together with the most approved practices of the two preceding administrations of Washington and Adams, and the committees of Congress under the articles of confederation. Several new provisions were also added, tending to render the system more perfect. These provisions are designed to regulate the trade—to preserve peace and to cultivate friendship—to secure the Indians against depredations on their hunting grounds—to define the boundary lines between them and the United States, and to promote their civilization by authorizing the executive to furnish them domestic animals, implements of husbandry, goods or money to the amount of $15,000 annually. The act also provides for the appointment of agents, and designates the manner in which licences and passports shall be granted, and breaches of the law punished. It interposes obstacles to the acquisition of Indian property, making it penal to buy a horse without a permit, or to take any article of dress, &c. in pledge for debt It authorises the president to take measures to restrain or exclude the introduction of ardent spirits into the Indian country, giving the agents summary powers of seizure ; and contains several subordinate provisions, tending to guide officers in the execution of their duties, and at the same time to protect the Indian in the exercise of his acknowledged rights.

In 1816, during the administration of Mr Madison, this act was amended by restricting the trade exclusively to citizens of the United States, under the penalty of forfeiture of the goods and furs, &c. A fine of one thousand dollars is also imposed upon any foreigner who shall visit the Indian territories without a passport, and the president is authorized to use the military force, should it become necessary to effect seizures of persons or property.

In 1822, during the presidency of Mr Monroe, an act further amendatory, and repealing certain provisions of the act of 1802, was passed. By the first section of which, licences, under bond, are authorized to be granted by the superintendents and agents, for a period not exceeding seven years for persons trading "with the remote tribes beyond the Mississippi, and two years for the trade with all other tribes." In explanation of the powers conveyed by one of the sections of the amended act, the president is authorized to direct Indian agents, Governors of territories acting as superintendents, and officers commanding frontier posts, to cause searches of the boats and packages of traders to be made under suspicion or information that ardent spirits is concealed for the purpose of being introduced into the Indian country. All purchase of goods intended as gifts or annuities are directed to be made by the agents and superintendents within their respective jurisdictions, who are required to settle their accounts properly vouched annually on the 1st of September, at the War Department, copies of which must be laid before Congress at the commencement of each session by the proper officer of the treasury department, specifying the names of all persons employed, the amount of goods or money paid out, the object of the expenditure, &c. In all trials respecting the right of property, this act, throws the burden of proof upon the white person, in every case where the Indian makes out a presumption of title in himself. The president is authorised to appoint, with the advice and consent of the Senate, a superintendent for Indian affairs to reside at St Louis, whose duties are confined to Indians frequenting that place, and an agent for the newly acquired territory of Florida ; and he is authorised, from time to time, to require additional security, and in larger amounts, from all officers intrusted with the disbursement or application of public funds.

A question had early arisen as to the criminal jurisdiction of the United States Courts in the Indian country, which led to an act to provide for the punishment of offences committed within their boundaries, passed March 3, 1817. This act is not intended to affect any treaty stipulations between the government and the Indians, or to interfere in any criminal questions between Indians, whether of a national or individual character, but simply provides for the punishment of crimes in which either the party accusing, or accused is a white man, and it simply gives the necessary jurisdiction to the courts, without affecting the executive power to pardon or reprieve as the last resort.

In 1818, (April 16) Congress passed an act directing the manner of appointing Indian agents, who are required to be nominated by the president to the Senate, and approved in the manner of other officers Congress also (April 20, 1818) passed an act fixing the compensation to agents and factors, a law, which by reciting the stations at which agents and factors should be kept, had in practice, the effect to ascertain and fix their number. So we find no agent appointed after this date, without a specific law of Congress.

(XVI) Page 87 MOVEMENTS OF THE NORTH WESTERN INDIANS DURING THE LATE WAR.—Among the accidental causes of depopulation, affecting the north western Indians, in modern times, none, perhaps, since the ravages of the small pox in 1778, has had a greater effect, than the character and influence of Tecumseh, and his brother the Prophet. By addressing themselves to the prejudices of the Indians, they acquired an influence, which, sustained as it was, by the resources of a foreign government, was wielded to embody a large force which served to keep the frontiers in alarm. To provide for the support of the Indian bands who accompanied the British arms, (poorly and irregularly as they were in fact, supported,) required no inconsiderable effort. And when reverses came, they were abandoned to misery and suffering in all their complicated forms. After the surrender of Malden and the battle of the Thames, they were completely abandoned. It has been computed by persons who participated in the scenes, that for one Indian warrior who was killed in battle, ten died of the effects of exposure, scanty or defective provisions, or disease.

Efforts to assemble the Indians, were made by Tecumseh, through his brother the Prophet, as early as 1806. His views were enlarged, and he embraced in the plan of an Indian confederacy, the most remote, as well as contiguous tribes. Unsuccessful at first, and unsuccessful throughout among his own tribe the Shawnees, very few of whom adhered to him, he accomplished by perseverance, by assuming arts of popularity, by dispatching his rivals under charges of witchcraft, and by a fortunate juncture of circumstances, which he could not otherwise have effected. But in thus resuscitating Pontiac's plan, of driving the whites back upon their atlantic settlements, and resuming the use of the bow and arrow, he sealed the political fortunes of the Indians. Success could not have been expected, under any enlarged view of the subject, and defeat could not but be attended with a great declension of numbers. From this declension they have never been able to recover, and it is but applying the experience of the past, to the anticipations of the future, to predict, that they never will.

The Prophet, who is still living, having recently been permitted to rejoin his people within the United States, though very essential in carrying into effect the schemes of his ambitious brother, played but a secondary part in the political drama. He was, however, first distinguished, and it was some time before it was discovered that he was not the principal actor. Messengers were dispatched by the Prophet, to the north western tribes in 1807, with speeches, accompanied with the usual formalities, urging them to repair immediately to his rendezvous. On reaching *L'Arbre Croche*, the Shawnees, who were employed on this mission, returned, and a deputation of Ottawas was sent to convey the message to lake Superior. This deputation met Mr. Holl.day, a trader, at White Fish point, on his return from his wintering ground at *L'Ance*, accompanied by the Indians of that post. A council was immediately called, and the purport of the message explained. The Indians were told that the world was approaching its end, that, that part of the country would soon be without light, and the inhabitants would be left to grope their way in total darkness, and that the only spot where they would be able to distinguish objects was the Prophet's position near Greenville. But that, previous to this calamity, the snow would fall, the next ensuing winter, as deep as the tops of the trees.

They were further told, to discontinue the use of every thing, which had been introduced among them by the whites. They were urged to discontinue the use of guns, and to resume the bow, to throw away their fire steels, and to obtain fire by the ancient method. They were forbid the use of ardent spirits, and tobacco, except the mild kind of tobacco, or smoking mixture, used in primitive times. All white men who had taken Indian wives were required to separate from them, and the women were summoned' with their children, to attend a general meeting of all the Indian tribes. Many cogent arguments were used, to induce the Indians to refrain from the use of civilised manufactures, to revert to their primitive customs, and to repair to the Prophet's station. To render all this more plausible and acceptable, the Prophet told them that he should induce the God of the Indians, to dispel the darkness. When this was accomplished, he informed them, that the animals would come forth plentifully out of the earth—that the Indians would afterwards be greatly multiplied in numbers and increase in strength, and finally live a life of ease and happiness.

The credulous Indians flocked from all quarters to obey this summons, which was delivered at the place above mentioned about the last of June. They immediately prepared to go off, and continued to press on, towards the Prophet's station until August, when the whole southern shores of lake Superior were depopulated. So complete was this desertion, that the traders who had proceeded a part of the way, to their wintering grounds, were compelled to return. Of a band of sixty hunters at L'Ance Kewgwinon, fifty nine went off, and of this number twenty five died of hunger and want, before the party returned. Similar instances of desertion occurred at Ontonagon, lac des Flambeau, Ottawa lake, Lapointe, St Croix river, &c and similar instances of the hardships they suffered, and the losses they sustained, might be enumerated. Not less than *eight hundred persons*, it is estimated, went from the vicinity of lake Superior, of whom, it is believed, that at least *one third*, died on the way.

When they reached the Prophet's town, they found that a war against the whites was proposed, and it was soon intimated that the Americans were the objects against whom the wrath of the Indians was to be directed. The Chippewas began to struggle back in the autumn. Some of them reached their homes in February and March and before the spring closed, all that hunger and disease had spared of the remainder arrived. But they were greatly emaciated, and miserably clad, and sunk in spirits.

From the depopulation thus produced the country did not recover before the war of 1812. to prepare them for which, had been the chief, but concealed object, of the Prophet and Tecumseh's early and strenuous exertions. The misery endured in the expedition to Ohio, was, however, fresh in their recollection, and prevented many from repairing to the principal scene of action. A comparatively small body of the northern Chippewas attended the operations of the British army about Detroit. The first service in which they participated, was the attack on Michilimackinac. About 300 Chippewas were mustered by the Agents of the North West Company, to accompany the expedition sent against that place from St. Joseph's. The fort of Mackinac being carried by surprise, by a party of regulars under Capt Roberts, with the French militia and voyageurs, many of the Indians did not arrive until two days after the surrender. And the greater part of them soon returned.

After the fall of Detroit, Shinwakonce led a party of about twenty five men, composed of warriors from St Mary's and Grand Island to Malden. This party participated in various skirmishes, and was present in the decisive battle on the Thames when a number of them were slain.

Shortly after the departure of this party, a larger body of men from Flambeau lake and adjacent villages, assembled at Sault Ste Marie, and set out to follow Shingwakonce. This band had not proceeded farther than the foot of lake Huron, when an alarming sickness broke out among them. One or two persons died, and the rest fled back in a panic.

On the upper Mississippi, a simultaneous movement took place among the Indians, but the exertions of the agents of the British government were not equally successful among the different tribes. Of the Sioux nation, only thirty warriors could be prevailed upon to go. They were led by Col. Robert Dickson, but were under the more immediate command of the Red Wing's son. Of this party, who were present in the unsuccessful attacks on forts Meigs and St. Stephens, not one was killed in battle, and one only wounded. This was Wanita, the chief since celebrated as a war leader of the Yancktons. He was shot through the body in so dangerous a manner, that the English surgeon, who was called to examine the wound, pronounced it incurable. In consequence, his father, who was present, took the son to his tent, and succeeded in effecting a complete cure. Wabisha, and his band, did not leave the waters of the Mississippi.

Of the Winnebagoes, there were present at Detroit, three hundred men; of the Menomonies, four hundred, the latter comprising the entire strength of the Menomonie nation. Many of the latter were killed in battle, but more died of wounds, or from diseases caused by exposure, fatigue, &c. The Sioux went back, after the defeat of Proctor at Sandusky, the other Indians remained.

The arguments used to induce the western Indians to join in a war against the Americans, were well calculated to produce the intended effect. They were told that the Americans, who were intruders upon their lands, were to be driven back—that they would never terminate the war, until the Americans were driven over the Allegany mountains. That, after this event, the Indians should be put into possession of their ancient hunting grounds, and placed under the protection of the British Government, who would guaranty their independence.* That, they should recieve annually from the British government, supplies of arms, ammunition, clothing, and provisions. That those warriors who distinguished themselves by their bravery, should be rewarded by *very large medals*, to be sent over by the King, for that purpose, &c. These promises were confirmed by a large wampum belt, upon which the tomahawk, and other war devices, were worked. This belt was passed from tribe to tribe, and village to village, that every warrior might lay his hands upon it. It was accompanied, with presents of tobacco, and the customary ceremonials. And had not the interests of the fur trade in that quarter, clashed with the business of war, it is highly probable that a much greater force, particularly of Sioux warriors, would have accepted the invitation, and joined the British forces at Malden. That so few of the Mississippi Indians joined them, is however, in some degree attributable to the comparatively small influence possessed by Tecumseh and the Prophet, over these tribes, they were not personally known, and among whom, it is probable, the reports of Shawnee miracles, were received with less conclusive weight.

Peace was concluded at the close of 1814, unknown to the Indians. Michilimackinac was given up. St. Josephs had been taken and demolished by Col. Croghan. The British authorities, upon that frontier, withdrew to a large uninhabited island of lake Huron contiguous to the passage into lake Superior, to which they gave the name of "Drummond." A large body of Indians repaired to the new station in the spring of 1815. Wabisha, and his son were among the number. This venerable Sioux

---

*A proposition of this kind was made by the British Commissioners at the treaty of Ghent.

chief, was received with marked attention, due no less to his character and influence, than to his age. A number of presents were laid before him.

My father! said he, addressing Col. M'Douall then commanding the post, What is this, I see before me? A few knives and blankets! Is this all you promised us, at the beginning of war? Where are those promises you made us at Michilimackinac, and sent to our villages on the Mississippi? You told us, you would never let fall the hatchet, till the Americans were driven beyond the Alleganies. That we should again be put into possession of our ancient hunting grounds, and that our British father would never make peace without consulting his red children. Has this come to pass? We never knew of the peace. We are now told that it was made by our Great Father beyond the Big waters, without the knowledge of his war chiefs here. That it is your duty to obey his orders. What is this to us! Will these paltry presents pay for the men we have lost, both in battle and upon the road? Will they soothe the feelings of our friends? Will they make good your *promises?*

For myself, I am an old man. I have lived long, and always found the means of supporting myself, and I can do so still. Perhaps my young men may pick up the presents you have laid before me. I do not want them.*

Since writing the foregoing, we have received the following remarks, from Dr Zina Pitcher, Surgeon U. S Army, whose opportunities of personal observation upon the character and diseases of the Indians, have been favorable.

"In your note on the subject of the diminution in numbers of our aboriginal neighbors, you have seized upon the most conspicuous, and, during their continuance, the most fatal causes of their national decline. With the small pox, you might however, associate the measels, which in consequence of their manner of treating the fever preceding the eruption, viz. the use of vapor and cold bath combined, most commonly tends to a mortal termination. To these two evils, propagated by the diffusion of a specific virus, may be added the prevalence of general epidemics, such as influenza, &c whose virulence expends its force without restraint upon the Indians. They are not, (as you are aware) a people who draw much instruction from the school of experience, particularly in the department of medicine, and when by the side of this fact, you place that of the protœan forms which the diseases of epidemic seasons assume, the inference must follow, that multitudes of them perish where the civilized man would escape, (of which I could furnish examples.)

"It is the province of the science of medicine to preserve to society its feeble and invalid members, which notwithstanding the war it wages upon the principles of political economists, augments considerably, the sum of human life. The victims of the diseases of civilization do not balance the casualties, &c, of a ruder state of society, as may be seen by inspecting the tables of the rates of mortality for a century past. These two last circumstances or facts, though they come within the scope of your quotation from Mr. Jefferson, are not specified in his remarks.

"I will suggest to you the propriety of improving this opportunity for setting the public right, on one point connected with the subject of your note, and this is, the effects of aboriginal manners upon their physical character. For my part, I have long since ceased to believe that they are indebted to their mode of life for the vigor, as a race, which they exhibit, but that the naturally feeble are destroyed by the vicissitudes to which

---

*Some of the data embraced in this note, have been used by a friend, to whom they were furnished, in an article in the North American Review.

they are exposed, and which, in fact, gives them an appearance hardy and athletic above their more civilized neighbors.

"Some of the causes above alluded to, being comparatively steady in their operation, must retard considerably the increase, if not positively diminish population."

(XVII) Page 88. The following anecdote was related to me by the late Col. Robert Dickson

"I was encamped on the Rocky island in Sturgeon Bay (of Green Bay) when the Indians invited me to be a spectator of their necromantic ceremonies Among many tricks which could be easily accounted for, I saw the following extraordinary scene Six Indians, having raised a large bon fire, at one instant jumped into the center of it, and the fire was immediately extinguished Afterwards, one of them put his arms into a large kettle of boiling water, and took out the beef In neither instance was any injury sustained "

This seems to prove, what has been asserted, that the Indians have the knowledge of plants, whose juice renders the body insensible to the effects of heat. And we think the island referred to, may be expected to yield this plant to the future botanist

(XVIII) Page 83 THE INDIAN WITHOUT CIVILIZATION BECAUSE WITHOUT CHRISTIANITY —To the traveller who visits the Indian country for information, to the man of business, who casually passes through it, or to the christian teacher who is actuated by more exalted motives, no object presents itself so forcibly to the mind, as the impoverished, unique, and fate-ridden Indian. We observe in them, the moral problem of a race, who have existed for centuries, in contact with a people differing from them, in all that constitutes physical and intellectual distinction, without having embraced, in any visible degree, manners, opinions and modes of life, urged upon by precept and example or without having lost, any of the essential traits, which mark them as a peculiar people We see the lean and cautious hunter, directing his stealthy footsteps in search of game, with the unaltered feeling and expectation, that God has provided for his sustenance, in this peculiar way, and that any efforts of his own, to change the mode, by agriculture or civilized arts, would be wrong, and was never intended We see the warrior, smeared with pigments and decorated with trinkets and feathers, captivated by the ceremonies of the war dance, and panting for the only species of honorable distinction known to his forefathers. We see the Indian jugeler and priest, exercising alternately the duties of a prophet and a physician, and rivetting the attention of his credulous listeners If we examine, the precincts of the houshold lodge, we find the consecrated sack, containing charmed medicines If we visit the abode of the sick, we find offerings to an invisible agency of spirits. as peculiar and multiform, in their character and office, as ever were invented by Rabbinical authority If we visit the graves of the dead, we find the idea of materiality throwing its grovelling fetters around the disembodied soul, in the food deposited upon the grave, and the implements buried within it.

In all this, there is little to distinguish the Indian of 1834 from the Indian of 1534.* Both exhibit the same natural endurance for suffering and stoical indifference to pain, the same passion for war, and aversion to industrious employments, and the same stubborn belief that they are the care of a

---
* The date of Cartier's first visit to Canada.

peculiar Creator who has set a mark between the white and red man, an opinion which has cost them so many battles and defeats, and led to such an accumulation of miseries, domestic and national. There is indeed, a doggedness of devotion, in this expectation, which may be compared to the reckless and desperate hope of the defenders of Jerusalem, when the Lord had visibly departed from the sanctuary.

As respects the mere external man, we have effected all that has been accomplished. We have clothed him in a robe of woolens instead of furs. We have put a gun into his hands, and taught him the use of an art of taking life, infinitely more destructive and prejudicial to the race of large animals, than the bow and arrow. We have supplied him with iron, instead of stone axes; and with silver instead of copper ornaments. We have taught him a new and expeditious mode of striking fire, and supplied him with metallic cooking vessels and knives. Could we stop here, we should stop within the limits of positive utility. But truth requires us to proceed. We have suplied him also with ardent spirits, instead of water, and thus established the most effectual barrier to every improvement.

Amid the rapid declenson of numbers, which this article has been a prominent cause in affecting, he has evinced, it is true, no absolute change of characteristic mental habits. The imbecility and prostration, resulting from its occasional use have uniformly been followed by recurrence to pre-existing trains of thought. But where the influence of the poison drug, has never been felt, there has not been a less marked hostility to the incipient steps of civilization. Philanthropy can not always console itself that the efforts it has bestowed upon the remote and sober bands have elicited results more particularly favorable to improvement. Religion has met the firmest opposition on the ground that the system of christianity, was not designed for them. And education has found the same impediment, for they have, from the beginning, regarded letters as the appropriate gift of the European race.

"And all well suited to their weal and woe,
"But which he knows not, nor desires to know."

Whenever these bands have been called upon, for opinions, by which the conduct of life is regulated, or passion and prejudice governed, we have found the primeval character of the mind, unchanged. A single act of Pontiac or Tecumseh, has done more to preserve their original modes of thinking and acting, than the whole course of the consistent christian lives of a Henry Obookiah or a Catherine Brown.

Labor in every aspect has appeared to our Indians, to be degrading. "I have never" said an Indian chief at Michilimackinac, who wished to concentrate the points of his honor, "I have never run before an enemy. I have never cut wood or carried water. I have never been disgraced with a blow. I am free as my fathers were before me."

The frigid apathy, with which they appear, thus far to have contemplated their fate, has been deemed surprising. But without a proper examination of the question, for it is a subject of just surprise, that he who is prepared to submit to a death of physical torture, should feel any strong compunctions in the prospect of want? There is a principle in the human heart, which renders the Indian callous to the future. And it need not be sought, we apprehend, in any thing more remote and deeply hidden, than the natural pride and love of indolence which are peculiar to that organ in its unsanctified and natural state.

Hitherto the question of their conversion and civilization has not been pressed upon the tribes with a steady and general force. They too, have had lands in plenty to hunt upon, and forests without measure to flee to.

But the topic that has lain dormant, as it were, for three centuries, is at last become a living and pressingly important one. It has particularly become so, within the present century. And the Indians, reproached as they have been, for want of foresight, are beginning to see and feel, that their condition is alarming. Some of the tribes have met the crisis. Others are beginning to consider it. While a large portion embracing the northern Indians, are indifferent on the subject. The fate which has overtaken others, will however soon overtake them. They must prepare for it. Christianity and civilization stand ready to aid them. The question lies between these and Paganism. They must embrace the former or be destroyed.

The following speech, illustrative of these opinions, was made by a Chippewa chief at Yellow Lake, in the spring of 1834, the day after the tribe had come to a decision adverse to the location of a mission among them. It was addressed to a missionary.

"Look at these three (Arabens, Maiengans, Bromais). To them belong the land. Since yesterday we have altered our mind. We have considered the subject. Listen to us. The same good spirit that made you white made us red. He gave you your religion, understanding, manners and customs, and land, and all you have. So he did ours to us. Before we saw the white men we used skins for dress, and cooked with stones. But, *after you had found our land on the map, you came.* Since that time the white men have always taken care of us. They have clothed us, and therefore we will never say or do any thing bad to them. Why should we therefore send you away. We ourselves would be sufferers. All of us tell you to stay. We again say stay. We do not wish you to go. We say to you stay. But we do not give you the land as yours. You may use them while you stay. You may plant, cut wood and timber, but when you go, it is ours."

K

DISCOURSE

DELIVERED BEFORE THE HISTORICAL SOCIETY OF MICHIGAN:

BY HENRY WHITING.

Cession of the Indian title to the United States—Building of Fort Recovery—Defeat of the Indians at the Maumee—Project of Whitney and Randall for purchasing a portion of the Indian Territory—Establishment of a Territorial Government—Destruction of Detroit by fire—Appointment of General Hull to the Northwestern command—Commencement of the war in 1812—Surrender of Detroit by Gen. Hull—An investigation of the conduct of Gen. Hull—Evacuation of Chicago—Surrender of Capt. Heald—Notice of Capt. Wells—Expedition under Gen. Harrison—Departure and Capture of Gen. Winchester—Massacre at the River Raisin—Victory of Commodore Perry—Expedition against Mackinac.

DISCOURSE.

GENTLEMEN OF THE HISTORICAL SOCIETY:

The first settlement, and early history of Michigan, have already been detailed by one of my predecessors; I shall therefore begin at a later period, and reviewing such events of character and importance as have had an influence on its destiny, and trace them down to the close of the late war.

The treaty of 1783, which terminated the war of the Revolution, included Michigan within the boundaries of the United States. It continued, however, under the dominion of Great Britain for some years after that date. But, preparatory to taking possession of it, and in order to avoid collision with the Indian tribes which owned the soil, a treaty was held with them by General Clark, at Fort M'Intosh, in 1785, by which they ceded their title to all lands lying within a line drawn from the mouth of the river Raisin, to a point six miles above, and thence running at that distance from the shore of Lake Erie and the river Detroit, until it should strike Lake St. Clair. At Fort Harmar, two years subsequently, the Island of Michilimackinac, with a circumference of twelve miles, was ceded in the same manner.

But the Territory thus secured by a treaty with Great

Britain, and with the Indian tribes of which we had thus established an amicable understanding, was many years sequestered from our possession. The cause, as well as the general consequences, of this international difficulty, are familiar to every reader of history, and do not come within the scope of this address. But the intimate relation which General Wayne's campaign of 1794 had with the formal surrender of the country to its rightful proprietor, makes it an essential part of the history, which it is the object of this society to embody. His operations were beyond the boundary of Michigan, but the results may be said to have determined its subsequent destiny.

Towards the close of the year 1793, General Wayne* re-occupied the ground which had been rendered memorable by the disastrous defeat of St. Clair, three years before, and there built a stockade work, which was significantly called Fort Recovery. While engaged in this labor, he offered a small reward for every human skull which should be found on the battle ground. More than five hundred of these relics of carnage are said to have been collected, and entombed beneath one of the Block-Houses of the work.

Leaving a suitable garrison at Fort Recovery, General Wayne returned to Fort Jefferson, and wintered there with the main body of his army. He had already been admonished that an active, dexterous and powerful enemy was in the wilderness surrounding him; for, while advancing towards Fort Jefferson, his rear guard had been attacked and entirely discomfited. In June 1794, before the army had left its winter quarters, a detachment, which had been to Fort Recovery as an escort of provisions, fell

---

*For the principal details of General Wayne's campaign, I am mainly indebted to a Manuscript Journal of Brigadier General Brady, of the United States Army, who began his long and serviceable and honorable military career as a Lieutenant, in that campaign.

into an ambush of Indians about a mile from the Fort, and was driven back with great loss; the victors continuing the pursuit to the very gates which they endeavored to enter with the fugitives.

On the 4th of July, 1794, General Wayne began his march from Fort Recovery, and took up the track of the Indians, who had left it obviously marked in their rear, either from the haste with which they made it, or, what is more probable, because they were desirous of luring him still farther into the recesses of the wilderness. At the crossing of the St. Mary's river, Fort Adams was built; and during the halt there, a man belonging to the Contractor's Department, deserted to the Indians, and carried to them the information of the movements of the army. In consequence of this notice, General Wayne, when he arrived at the confluence of the Anglaise with the Maumee, found their villages abandoned. Several days were spent at this place in building Fort Defiance, and awaiting the return of a small party of spies, which, under the direction of Capt. Wells, had been sent forward to reconnoitre the enemy. This skilful and intrepid warrior of the woods, led his party within so short a distance of the British works, as to ascertain that the Indians were encamped under its protection. He took one or two prisoners, and made a bold though unsuccessful attempt on a camp of warriors in the night, in which he was wounded. Soon after his return, the army moved slowly and cautiously down the left bank of the Maumee. During the march, General Wayne despatched messengers of peace to the Indians, in the hope that a battle might still be avoided. On the 19th of August, he reached the Rapids, about four miles above the British Post. He there erected a small work for the protection of his baggage and stores, and on the 20th again advanced.

The British Post had been occupied by a garrison sent from Detroit the previous spring. There could be no misapprehension of the motives which led to this occupation, taking place as it did, several years after the treaty by which the country had been ceded to the United States, and at a time too, when the angry and protracted negociation of several years, relating to it, was supposed to be about to terminate in an open rupture. The Indians were all decidedly in favor of the British. With the jealousy natural to weakness, they were always prone to array themselves against the power which most directly pressed upon their destinies, and which they thought most likely to affect them injuriously. The British were fully aware of this feeling, which their agents were zealously active to excite and foster. They saw in it the means of crippling the growth of a young rival, who was stretching out into the west with giant strides, and trampling down the forest on every side. The country had been ceded and secured by a treaty still in force; but new negociations were then going on under the influence of several disastrous defeats, and as the Indians demanded an independent dominion over the country in dispute, the British government might expect that a surrender, so desirable to them, would at last be granted. A proposition of a similar character was made by the same government towards the close of the last war. The entire independence of the Indians occupying a wide belt on our north-western frontiers, was formally and seriously demanded, as one of the conditions of peace.

As long as the formidable coalition of tribes which General Wayne found in arms, should continue united and hostile, it was evident that the British pretensions and hopes would remain. It was therefore, of great moment with Gen'l Wayne, and with his country, that his present steps should be taken with the utmost prudence. A new defeat, like that which had terminated almost every previous campaign, would have proved, not only destructive to his army, so far advanced in the wilderness, but probably decided the British to openly espouse the cause of the Indians. General Wayne, in the present case, could feel no assurance that this cause would not then be sustained by such co-operation as the Fort and Garrison could afford. Indeed, the position of the Indians, under the walls of the Fort, rendered it probable that such a course had been determined on. In that event, it is said that General Wayne had instructions to act offensively against the Post. There does not, however, appear to be any testimony to this surmise on record. But it is not necessary; for under such circumstances, no other authority would have been required, than the ordinary and acknowledged rules of warfare. If the British Garrison had been found by General Wayne actually co-operating with the Indians, it would at once have become equally obnoxious with them to his hostility, and as legitimate an object of attack.

General Wayne had about three thousand men under his command, and the Indians are computed to have been equally numerous. This is not improbable, as the hostile league embraced the whole North-Western frontier. As he approached the position of the enemy, he sent forward a battalion of mounted riflemen, which was ordered, in case of an attack, to make a retreat in feigned confusion, in order to draw the Indians on more disadvantageous ground. As was anticipated, this advance soon met the enemy, and being fired on, fell back, and was warmly pursued toward the main body.

The morning was rainy, and the drums could not communicate the concerted signals with sufficient distinctness. A plan of turning the right flank of the Indians was not therefore fulfilled. But the victory was complete, the whole Indian line, after a severe contest, giving way, and flying in disorder. About one hundred savages were killed.

During the action and subsequently, while General Wayne remained in the vicinity of the British, there did not appear to be any intercourse between the garrison and the savages. The gates were kept shut against them, and their route and slaughter were witnessed from the walls with apparent unconcern, and without offering any interposition or assistance. After the battle, General Wayne devastated all the fields, and burnt all the dwellings around the Fort, some of them immediately under the walls. The house of Col. M'Kee, an Indian trader, who was supposed to have exercised great influence over the Indians, was reduced to ashes in the general conflagration. During this work of desolation, a correspondence took place between General Wayne and Major Campbell, the British commandant, which inevitably assumed a somewhat belligerant character: but the prudent forbearance of the latter, who concluded not to extend his interference beyond remonstrance, averted an attack on himself, which would have followed any more serious or efficacious opposition.

That the Indians did not expect to find such luke-warmness in their Anglo-friends, and even that they regarded the Fort as a refuge in case of misfortune, is probable from the circumstances of the case, and rendered almost unquestionable, by the well known reproach of Tecumseh, in his celebrated speech to General Proctor, soon after Perry's victory in 1813.

After remaining in the neighborhood of the Fort three days, General Wayne retired by easy marches, to Fort Defiance, destroying the Indian corn-fields, which were spread over the rich bottoms of the Maumee, in his progress. This measure of stern hostility, was justified by the probability, that fear of famine would be a powerful auxiliary in producing peace. The morning before the army made this retrogade movement, General Wayne, after arranging his force in such a manner as to show that they were all on the alert, advanced with his numerous staff and a small body of cavalry, to the glacis of the British Post, reconnoitering it with great deliberation, while the garrison were seen with matches lighted, and all prepared for any emergency. It is said that General Wayne's party overheard one of the British subordinate officers, who appealed to Major Campbell for permission to fire on the cavalcade, and avenge such an insulting parade under his Majesty's guns. But it appears that the British commandant restrained his loyal indignation, and suffered the American General to retire unharmed from a reconnoisance, which, had it encountered less forbearance, might have given a new proof how truly he merited the popular name of "mad Anthony."

Leaving Major Hunt in command of Fort Defiance, General Wayne moved still higher up the river to the old Miami towns, where he built Fort Wayne. Col. Hamtramck was left at this Post, and General Wayne returned with the main body of the army to Greenville. The campaign lasted about three months, and resulted in a most signal overthrow of the Indians, and, what was perhaps of more importance the future peace of the country—of the insiduous schemes of the British Government. Several posts were established in the hostile region, securing the ground which had been gained, and admonishing the Indians that it would be prudent to submit to a power which had gained ascendency over them too formidable to be resisted.

The treaty of Greenville was not concluded until the following August; but it does not appear that any active hostilities troubled the frontiers during the intermediate period. Jay's treaty, which adjusted our difficulties with Great Britain, at least as far as related to the Indian country, had occurred in the mean time, and, leaving the tribes little or no hope of foreign co-operation, disposed them to a general peace.

The articles of the treaty of Greenville which relates to Michigan, recapitulated with some enlargement, the substance of the previous treaties. The belt, or strip, of six miles width, reaching from the river Raisin to Lake St. Clair, and several local cessions, still confined the scope for a white population to within very narrow limits. But the most sanguine mind did not probably then anticipate the time when there would be a necessity to enlarge that scope. The country had been deemed important for military occupation, and for the fur trade; it was still regarded in no other light; and the wildest prophesy did not venture to predict a more exalted destiny.

Between the ratification and execution of Jay's treaty, a scheme, most vitally affecting the fortunes of Michigan, was concerted between two or three adventurous projectors from the States, and a number of merchants or traders at Detroit, which, although eventuating in a failure, was too ambitious and exorbitant, not too deserve a record among the singular incidents that marked its early history. During the session of Congress held in 1795, Robert Randall of Pennsylvania, and Charles Whitney of Vermont were taken into custody by the House, for "an unwarrantable attempt to corrupt the integrity of its members." This Robert Randall, in pursuit of some object in which he failed, visited Detroit, where his inventive genius unfolded to him a new and more magnificent plan of improving his fortunes. In conjunction with Charles Whitney, and one other person, he entered into an agreement with seven merchants residing at or near Detroit, by which the parties bound themselves to obtain a preemption right from the United States, of a certain Territory therein defined, which was to be afterwards purchased of the Indians. This Territory contained, as it was conjectured, from eighteen to twenty millions acres, and was embraced by the Lakes Erie, Huron, and Michigan. Six members of Congress deposed before that body, that Randall and Whitney had, at several times and places, unfolded to them their scheme, by which it appeared that the Territory in question was to be divided into forty-one shares, five of which were to belong to the traders at Detroit, who were parties to the agreement,—six to be appropriated to Randall and his associates,—and the other twenty-four to be equally divided between such northern and southern members of Congress, as should by their votes or exertions, secure the enactment of the law necessary to promote the project. The amount proposed to be paid to the United States for the right to make this purchase of the Indians, was from a half to a million of dollars. The merchants who were associated, were represented to have such influence over the Indians, as to render feasible the purchase of their title to the soil. To the suggestion made by some members, that the late treaty opposed a bar, as it reserved to the United States exclusively this preemption right, it was alleged that the Indians were dissatisfied with the terms of the treaty, and would not abide by them; and that this plan would appease them, and secure tranquility throughout that section of the country.

The more particular details of this extraordinary project, are recorded in the Journal of the House of Representatives, by which it appears that, after having been kept in custody some time, and subjected to an examination at the bar of the House, Whitney was discharged without punishment, while Randall received a public reprimand from the

Speaker, and was obliged to pay the fees which had accrued in his case.

It would be useless to hazard conjectures as to the effect which a more successful prosecution of this enterprise would have had on the fortunes of this Territory. Falling under the control of a few large proprietors, the progress of settlement might have been accelerated or retarded, according to the ability with which it was conducted. The state of weakness and pupilage, which kept the wilderness of Michigan intact and intangible for more than twenty years, might have been suddenly converted into a vigorous growth of population, by the active management of an association, deeply interested in its advancement and prosperity; or, what is more probable the immigration which has been within a few years flowing into the Peninsula, and has already filled the interior with thriving villages and farms, might have been repulsed or checked by the illiberality or cupidity of a proprietory despotism.

The possession of the Territory in 1796, immediately extended over it the ordinance of 1787, which was already in operation in the North-Western Territory, within whose limits Michigan was embraced. Though small in population, yet its inconvenient remoteness from the centre of the territorial government, which was at Cincinnati, was severely felt. The erection of this into a state did not mitigate the condition of Michigan in this respect. She was still as far from the central government as ever, and every political inconvenience remained unchanged.

January 11, 1805, Indiana being erected into a separate state, the residue of the North-Western Territory was divided into two Territories, Illinois and Michigan; and on the 1st July, the same year, the territorial government of the latter was organised at Detroit by General William Hull, the newly appointed Governor. On the 11th of the previous June, Detroit had been destroyed by fire. Having been built amid a savage and often hostile population, Detroit like most frontier places, had been compressed within a very small compass, having streets which scarcely exceeded the breadth of common alleys, and the whole surrounded by a stockade. The Fort* was on the outside of this stockade, and behind the town. The buildings were of wood, and contiguous to each other, and being for the most part old, were highly combustible. The fire broke out in a stable, about 10 o'clock in the morning. The atmosphere was calm at this time; but, as is common in such cases, the spreading flames soon created a wind, which at once fanned them into fury. At the end of three or four hours, but two buildings were standing, the one a store house† belonging to Mr. M'Intosh, the other a bake-house at the waters' edge. The entire population of the town was thus rendered houseless, and leaving the smouldering ruins, encamped on the commons in the rear. In this situation Governor Hull found his people. It was a melancholy commencement of his administration, and it was nearly as perplexing as melancholy. Impatient in their distresses under delay, some of the proprietors had begun to rebuild on the old sites, and thus to renew the town on its former cramped and inconvenient plan. Others were for appropriating at once the vacant commons without the stockade, to the benefit of the sufferers.

General Hull, immediately on his arrival, turned his attention to this urgent subject, and laid out the town in its present shape, subject to the approval of Congress. The

---

*This Fort was erected by Major Le Noult, in 177-, when Detroit was threatened by General Clarke from Vincennes. It was called Fort Shelby after the late war; and was destroyed in 1827, the ground having been ceded by Congress to the town of Detroit.

† This store-house the last remnant of the old town was taken down in 1830.

arrangement of the plan has been attributed to Judge Woodward, one of the judges of the territorial court at that time. He regarded it as one that combined all the excellencies which could be culled from previous plans, from that of Constantinople to that of Washington city. It was upon a magnificent scale, and unfolded an outline which, he often declared, would require eight centuries to fill up. This was assigning an ample period for the consummation of almost any human project. But the plan, however admirable in theory, has proved inconvenient in practice. It has entailed embarrassment on the place, which will probably perpetuate the projector's name through a long posterity, but without those econiums which were perhaps anticipated. A less ambitious and innovating genius, would have followed the guide of William Penn, and thus have introduced simplicity, symmetry, and convenience, which now appear little else than excentricity, irregularity, and perplexity.

At this time, the land at the disposal of the government, or which could be appropriated to cultivation by the whites, was the narrow strip before alluded to, running from the River Raisin to Lake St. Clair. The policy of the French Government, while the country was in its possession, did not appear to aim at improvement of the soil. Settlements for agriculture was not therefore encouraged. Only a few grants of land were made, and traffic with the Indians for furs seems to have been the only object in view. The inhabitants became in some degree incorporated with the aborigines, and the wide spread interior was preserved as a waste, for the better propagation of the fur bearing animals. The English pursued a similar policy. No effort appears to have been made, while they occupied the country, to enlarge the boundaries of cultivation.

In November, 1807, Governor Hull held a treaty at Brownstown with the Peninsula Tribes, which added all the lands, not before possessed under former treaties, within a line running on the exterior or western side of the counties of Lenawe, Washtenaw, Shiawassa, and Sagana. But the lands thus acquired were not brought into market until the year 1817.

The new town of Detroit was without other defence, than the Fort in its rear, until 1807 or 8, when the threatening movements of some of the neighboring tribes of Indians, led to the erection of a stockade around it, which was not removed until 1817.

The Territory of Michigan, though on the skirts of the United States, and, by its remoteness from the coast, would seem to have been almost independent of the effect of a war with Great Britain, yet, by an inauspicious train of events, she was made almost the first victim of that which broke out in 1812. Previous to the declaration of war, but while that Congress was in session which made it, Governor Hull was in Washington. A plan appears to have been concerted while he was there, having that event in anticipation. His knowledge of the North-western frontier, combined with his civil position, which gave him control over many of its resources, made it expedient to vest him with military command. He was accordingly appointed a Brigadier General in the army of the United States. In justification of this appointment—the propriety of which the public was led, by subsequent events, much to question, it should be recollected, that Governor Hull left the Revolutionary army with the rank of Major, and a military reputation inferior to few officers of his grade, having frequently distinguished himself by his gallantry and good conduct in action, so as to receive the commendation of Washington in general orders. This appointment of Brigadier General he at first declined, and an officer, already in service, was selected for the North-western command. This officer, however, through sickness, or some other cause, not being able to assume it, Gov. Hull was induced to accept the appointment of Brigadier General; and in fulfilment of the plan of operations, immediately proceeded to Ohio, where the 4th regiment of Infantry, and a body of volunteers, were in readiness to receive his orders. With this force he commenced his march for Detroit. War had not then been declared, but the prospect of it was so immediate, that it would seem to have been the part of prudence to have acted with the same caution, as if it had been so. Contrary, however, to such a course, General Hull, on his arrival at Maumee, near lake Erie, freighted a vessel, which received the baggage and stores of the army, a few individuals, and also some important documents. This vessel sailed for Detroit, and took the usual passage into the Detroit river, which is by the way of Malden. The day after her departure, General Hull received official information of the declaration of war, and soon re-commenced his march for Detroit, where he arrived on the 9th of July.*

The vessel which had been sent from the Maumee, as it approached Malden, was captured by a detachment from the garrison at that place without resistance. It does not appear that the party on board was directed to be on its guard, or prepared for such an event. The British boarded the vessel, gave notice of hostilities, and took possession. Sent into the very jaws of the expected enemy, resistance with such means as were provided, would probably have been unavailing; but she might have been directed to take a less exposed channel, or fitted for the emergency which

---

* For many of the details of General Hull's campaign, and of the subsequent military incidents of the North western frontier, I am indebted to a memoir read before the Lyceum of Detroit, in 1819, by Major Rowland, who was an officer in the United States army, during the late war, and served on that frontier.

happened. Much insight into the intended operations of the Americans is said to have been obtained by this unlucky capture. It appears that the British had been some days apprized of our declaration of war. With a forecast eminently required at such critical conjunctures, the British diplomatists about Washington urged forward the eventful tidings to all their frontiers with the utmost alacrity; and every Post was so forewarned as to give it the advantage of initial operations. While, under existing circumstances, it was undoubtedly the duty of General Hull to have acted with the same heed as if war had actually been declared, yet, there can be no excuse for the tardy and blundering movements of the War Department, which suffered itself, in almost every instance, to be outstripped by the superior alertness of the enemy; and left almost the whole North-western frontier from Niagara to Prairie du Chien, with scarcely a precautionary intimation, to be vigilant and prepared for hostility.

On the 9th of July, General Hull received orders to cross the river Detroit, and take possession of Canada. His command had been impatient to make the movement, and had urged it upon him immediately after his arrival. At such a moment all procrastination was in favor of the enemy, as each day increased its strength, and diminished the chances of success. The garrison of Malden was at that time small, and without any immediate resource except from a few of the Canadian militia, who were rather reluctant and feeble auxiliaries,—and probably awaited only the approach of General Hull, whose force was comparatively overwhelming, to surrender.

Preparation having been made for the transit, General Hull took possession of the Canadian shore on the 12th July, and established his head quarters at Sandwich. The inhabitants were invited to come in and receive protection, which would ensure them the privileges of friends. Many were induced by the paramount dominion which the Americans appeared to possess over the country, and the probability that they would preserve it, to transfer their allegiance or, at least, to assume a neutrality.

Under pretext that heavy artillery was necessary to an attack on the fort at Malden, the army lay inactive at Sandwich from the 12th of July to the 8th of August. One or two detachments were sent out in the mean time, one of which, under the command of Colonel Cass, soon after the army crossed, drove in a picket stationed on the bridge over the river Canard, only a few miles from Malden, and took possession of it, advising General Hull of the movement, and recommending an immediate attack on that place. The recommendation was slighted, and the detachment ordered to return, leaving the enemy to reoccupy a station, highly important to either party, in the event of a future attack.

While these slothful and fruitless operations were going on below, the island of Michilimackinac above, had been captured by the enemy. The British at St. Joseph's having been promptly apprised of the rupture between the two countries, an expedition, consisting of a few regulars, some Canadian militia, and a large body of Indians, was immediately prepared against the post of Michilimackinac. Lieutenant Hanks, who commanded at that island, was first informed of hostilities, by a summons from the British commandant, under the walls of his Fort, to surrender. He at once submitted on honorable terms, having no reason to anticipate succor, and feeling unable long to hold out against such a force. It was perhaps fortunate that he obeyed the dictates of prudence rather than gallantry, as it appears by the semi-official communication of one of the British agents in the transaction, that the Indians were prepared to retaliate the slightest resistance with an indiscriminate massacre. The surrender took place on the 17th of July.

During General Hull's delay at Sandwich, within striking distance of Malden, General Brock, taking advantage of an adroit manœuvre of Sir George Prevost, who persuaded General Dearborn to enter into an armistice, which suspended all operations as high up as the Niagara frontier, moved up the province, to the relief of that place.

On the 9th of August, General Hull recrossed the river Detroit, and abandoned Canada, after an inglorious occupation of less than a month. The reasons alleged for taking this step—which appears to have been condemned by his army—were, that his communication with Ohio, the source of his supply of provisions, could not be easily maintained while he remained on the Canada side. He had likewise indirect information that General Brock, by some arrangement below, would be at liberty soon to assist, by strong succors, the upper Province. The news of the surrender of Michilimackinac, which would disengage the numerous northern tribes of Indians, also threw weight into the scale, already inclined to preponderate on the timid side. Previous to recrossing, General Hull had detached Major Van Horn with about two hundred men towards the river Raisin, to escort some provisions which were at that place on their route to Detroit. The detachment was surprised by a party of Indians near Brownstown, and retreated in disorder back to Detroit, leaving some dead on the field. The day on which the army recrossed, Colonel Miller, with another detachment, consisting of the 4th regiment and a body of militia, amounting to about 600 men, was sent down the river to remedy the disaster. About the middle of the afternoon, his advance guard under the command of Captain Snelling, met the enemy near Maguaga. This guard gallantly maintained its position until sustained by the main body, which was soon led up by Colonel Miller. The

British and Indians were posted behind a rude breastwork, thrown up in the woods. They were dislodged after a short contest, and retreated with precipitation to their boats, in which they crossed the river again, leaving the Americans undisputed masters of the field and the route to the river Raisin. But Colonel Miller was detained on the battle ground until the next day by the want of provisions, which were to have followed him. The next day he was ordered back to Detroit, the misapprehensions or timidity of the General having led him to believe that, although victorious, the detachment had gained no ground farther than "the points of their bayonets extended."* On the 13th instant, still having the safe arrival of the provisions at the river Raisin in view, Colonels M'Arthur and Cass were detached, by a back route, through the forest, on that service.

On the 14th of August, General Brock arrived at Malden with a reinforcement. With a promptitude characteristic of his bold and enterprising genius, he at once moved up to Sandwich; and on the 15th summoned General Hull to surrender. Regarding their relative strength, General Hull having the most numerous force—and their relative position, the two armies being separated by a broad and deep river,—such a summons wears the aspect of an empty gasconade. But General Brock had penetrated into the weakness of his opponent's character, and knew that even a gasconade could assail it with effect. Bespeaking confidence and spirit on one side, it would be likely to create distrust and despondency on the other. Such was the effect in the present instance, though not immediately displayed. The reply of General Hull was a decided negative, though accompanied by certain explanations which were

---

* Genearal Hull's letter to the Secretary of War.

not called for, and made in a tone of deprecation, which, if other evidence were wanting, might have instructed an intelligent enemy in the imbecility of his antagonist. Subsequent disclosures showed that General Brock did not want such evidence. On his arrival at Malden, with the tact of a skilful commander, he at once endeavoured to ascertain the character of the American General. It is said that the vessel captured at Malden contained much of his recent correspondence. The anxious and shrinking spirit which pervaded this correspondence, combined with the timid and procrastinating operations of General Hull, while he had a foothold in Canada, immediately convinced him, (as he afterwards frankly told an American officer of rank,)* that he had only to assume a front of boldness and decision, to insure an easy victory. It was thus, by that penetration and promptitude which belongs to gifted minds, that the British General saw and compassed a result, which could be accounted for by the world, only by supposing bribery on one side and treachery on the other. He did not attempt to tamper with an integrity which, we firmly believe, would have resisted all temptations of that nature with firmness and indignation; but he detected a weakness and irresolution which could be far more effectually and successfully assailed, and which at once gave his numerically equal force an overwhelming superiority.

As soon as General Brock received the answer of General Hull to his summons (the tenor of which he no doubt anticipated, as the most craven spirit waits for a sufficient and plausible excuse for yielding to its fears) a cannonade was opened on Detroit from batteries which had been suffered to be constructed without the least attempt at hindrance. It was returned by others, which had long been

---

* Governor (then Colonel) Cass.

in readiness on our side, but which had thus far been muzzled in silence. The position of a small vessel, belonging to the British, on the evening of the 15th rendered it probable that General Brock intended to cross the river at Springwells, either in the night, or early in the morning. To observe such a movement, Captain Snelling was sent with a small detachment to that point. Several officers recommended that a heavy piece of ordnance should be placed there, both to compel the vessel to remove, and to obstruct any attempt to cross. Much might have been effected by such a piece, which in the event of a necessity to abandon it, might have been dismounted and rendered temporarily unserviceable. But the detachment was ordered to return to Detroit by break of day, and General Brock made an early transit, with his whole force, without any molestation. He marched in column up the river road, having, according to the most impartial computation about one thousand men, including militia and Indians, who probably constituted nearly one half his numbers.

General Brock made a short halt at the small bridge about a mile below Detroit, and took breakfast there, as if awaiting the effects of the panic which his bold movements would probably strike in his opponent. Evidence of this was soon made manifest, General Hull's Aid being about this time sent over the river with a flag of truce. General Brock immediately sent forward a messenger to enquire the purpose of this flag. An answer was returned by General Hull, leading at once to the negociation, which soon terminated in a surrender.

While this interchange of messages was taking place, General Hull, at the suggestion of one of his staff, permitted arrangements to be made for defence without the Fort, which, had the battle been fought, as was then anticipated by every one, excepting perhaps General Hull himself, would have contributed much to a favorable result. The British were without artillery, and pursued a line of march, with the river on one flank, and orchards, enclosed by strong fences, affording excellent positions for annoyance and attack, on the other, exposing themselves with a daring recklessness, which nothing but a reliance on the imbecility of the enemy could have justified.

Instead of availing himself of any of these means of offence, General Hull seems to have avoided all possible collision, which might frustrate the capitulation then determined on. All the troops were withdrawn from the excellent positions they had taken, and ordered to concentrate within the Fort—already sufficiently garrisoned by the 4th regiment—as if from an apprehension, that, while there remained a chance of contact with the enemy, their ardor might burst forth without orders, and avert the disgrace which impended over them.

It does not appear that General Hull, in coming to the resolution of capitulating, took any other council than from his own fears. He hinted to the gallant Colonel Miller, who was then sick, his intention to send a flag, and when advised to consult his officers, said there was no time for consultation. General Brock, in his summons on the 15th, had introduced the very common threat, that in case a surrender was not immediately made, he could not answer for the conduct of his Indians, who might be exasperated by resistance. This empty menace may have shaken a mind, exhausted and sinking beneath the weight of responsibility and embarrassments; for the whole tenor of General Hull's conduct on the morning of the surrender, seems to have showed an excessive anxiety to avoid all hostility, which might give pretence for putting it in execution. Even while the articles were being signed, a British detachment is said to have approached the Fort, and scarcely waited until the

American flag had been struck, before it took possession. The articles of capitulation embraced the detachment under Colonel M'Arthur, which, although within striking distance of Detroit, was not known by General Hull to be in its neighborhood; and also, the party with Captain Brush at the river Raisin, nearly thirty miles distance. This sweep of all under his control within the vortex of surrender, may have proceeded from a morbid solicitude for their protection from Indian massacre, rather than from a wish to make the ruin as wide spread as possible. The first detachment, being too near to retreat with safety, submitted with the rest. That at the river Raisin, temporarily under the command of Captain Rowland, rejected the terms, and effected its retreat into Ohio.

Thus terminated General Hull's campaign on the north-western frontier. A disaster, in the very outset of the war of so serious and humiliating a character, threw a disheartening gloom over the whole country. It exhibited a weakness and insufficiency in our military management, strikingly and lamentably unsuited to the arduous struggle in which we had engaged. Awkwardness and imbecility seemed to pervade every Department from the War office to the very skirts of our operations. An overflowing measure of obloquy was cast upon General Hull in consequence of this event. Indignation and vituperation followed him into his captivity, and met him on his return to his country. He was soon after subjected to a trial, which after a most thorough, and as we have reason to believe, impartial investigation, resulted in awarding the extreme punishment of the law—a sentence of death. This sentence was accompanied by a recommendation to mercy, which of course prevailed with the President of the United States, on whose decision the prisoner's ultimate fate depended.

The lapse of time mellowed the asperity of opinion,

and when, on the brink of the grave, General Hull made an eloquent appeal from the judgment of the court which condemned him, he seems to have won, through conviction or compassion, many among his neighbors to a belief in his innocence. A public proof of this sentiment was given in Boston, which probably served to assuage the bitterness of his past lot, and to cast a gleam of sunshine on the short remnant of his days.

While we would not unnecessarily disturb the repose of his ashes, it is the duty of impartial history to examine into, and decide on an event, in which the public have a concern paramount to that of any individual. That General Hull stated the necessity of naval co-operation on Lake Erie, and that he deemed it essential to his success, may be fully admitted, and had there been the slightest forecast in the preparation for the north-western campaign, no doubt this important auxiliary would have been provided. Nothing but the same blindness and inefficiency which exposed every north-western post to capture, even before they were aware of the war, would have neglected so essential a part of the plan. But the immediate cause of General Hull's numerous failures, does not appear to be attributable to so remote a source. Notwithstanding the many difficulties he had to surmount in his march, he reached Detroit in safety, with a force fully adequate to effect the purposes directly in view. The upper Canadian Province was almost defenceless, having only a small detachment of troops at Malden, and a Fort which scarcely deserved the name. When he crossed into Canada, he not only met with no opposition, but found most of the inhabitants neutral, or positively friendly. Many pretexts have been urged to excuse the delay of an attack on Malden, which, we have every reason to presume, only waited the appearance of General Hull, with his army, to surrender. Such an event, although not of much importance, as the place was scarcely tenable, would have had the double effect of encouraging the Americans, and discouraging the British. And it might have prevented the movement of General Brock, who would probably have doubted the expediency of attempting a re-conquest of the upper Province with such a small force.

The return to Detroit, at a time when every object in Canada had been rendered nearly unattainable by delay and mismanagement, was perhaps a prudent step. An attack could have been made by General Brock on that side of the river with the chances of success greatly multiplied. The movement of Col. Miller towards the River Raisin, after the battle of Maguaga, could have been made without any probable molestation. The discomfiture of the British and Indians had been complete, and all obstructions were removed, at least for a time. Having effected the object in view, the whole army would have been concentrated at Detroit. The batteries opposite to Detroit were permitted to rise without any attempt at hindrance. Not even a gun (many of which were ready for effect) was allowed to be fired; and the suggestion of Major Jessup, to carry them by a nocturnal attack, was treated with neglect. The transit of General Brock at Springwells may not have been prevented by such a force as prudence would have placed at that distance from the main body. But even such a detachment as was on the spot, might have given much molestation, and caused some loss, especially if it had been assisted by a field piece. General Brock's march from that place towards the town, was continually exposed to obstacles, which the slightest generalship or enterprise would have rendered formidable. The approach to the Fort was lined with defences, which would have enabled resolute troops to dispute every inch of ground. The Fort itself was a strong, bastioned work, every way fitted for a short siege, and, after all obstacles had been removed, might for a time have defied the British, destitute, as they were, of artillery. The ramparts were in good repair, the ditches deep, and bristling with pickets; and the fourth Regiment alone was a garrison that could have resisted any coup de main. If provisions were not abundant, there was at least a present sufficiency, as well also as of ammunition.

When General Brock landed a Springwells, he was informed, by an Indian, of the approach of Col. M'Arthur's detachment in his rear; and he is said to have precipitated his march towards Detroit, lest the pevious arrival of this reinforcement should defeat his plans. Although there was no concert of action between Colonel M'Arthur and General Hull, as the latter appears to have been unapprised that the former was so near at hand, yet, had only a few hours resistance been maintained, this detachment would have come in as a powerful and probably decisive diversion in General Hull's favor.

Indeed, after the most thorough and impartial investigation of this disastrous event, it is difficult to avoid the conclusion, that it resulted from mismanagement and inefficiency; and that the exercise of ordinary generalship and spirit, would have converted those days of humiliation and sorrow, into days of triumph and rejoicing.

A provisional government was established by the British at Detroit, and a small force placed in the Fort. The Indians, who were numerous, and claimed large rewards for their co-operation, and who were but slightly, if at all restrained by the garrison, carried plunder and devastation into almost every house, and through almost every farm in the Territory. The miserable inhabitants had no alternative but to submit, or incur the hazard of more aggravated outrage. Most of the citizens of Detroit were sent into exile, and distress and ruin appeared to be the inevitable lot of all.

Contemporaneously with these events on the eastern side of the peninsula of Michigan, another disaster, rendered memorable by the folly which led to it, and the blood which accompanied it, occurred on the western side, under the walls of Chicago. While yet in Canada, General Hull, actuated, no doubt, by the apprehensions which made him regard all things under his control with trembling anxiety, sent orders to Captain Heald, who commanded at Chicago, to evacuate that Post, and retreat to Fort Wayne. Every order of this unfortunate General appeared to be pregnant with misfortune. That which was issued at this time to Captain Heald, involved a garrison, which had ample means of defence at its Post, in disgrace and blood. The order for evacuation was received on the 9th of August. Captain Wells, of the Indian department who, with a few faithful Miamies, was to guide the retreat, mistrusting the fidelity of the Pottawatamies, recommended an immediate evacuation, before that tribe should have time to concentrate around the Fort. His recommendation was disregarded, and, in a short time, more than four hundred of them had collected in the neighborhood. In order to secure their forbearance, a promise was made to them, that all the surplus stores should be left at their disposal. Captain Heald prudently foresaw that large quantities of whiskey and powder, such as were then on hand, might be dangerous gifts to the Indians, and resolved to destroy clandestinely as much of them as possible before the evacuation. He accordingly, during the nights, when the Indians were not present, threw most of the powder into a well, and wasted a greater part of the whiskey. The Indians are said to have obtained some intimation or knowledge of these nocturnal transactions; and, regarding them as an infringement on their rights, may have then conceived the plan of vengeance, which they afterwards so fearfully executed.

After the Pottawatamies had assembled in such numbers, both Captain Wells and Mr. Kenzie (who was an Indian Agent at the place and knew well the character and feelings of these Indians) represented to Captain Heald that a retreat would then be unsafe. But their representations had no effect. He had neglected to make it at a time when no obstacles were in the way, and by delaying in order to destroy the surplus whiskey and ammunition, had deprived himself of the means of remaining, when it had become prudent and proper to do so.

On the 15th of August, the garrison, consisting of 54 regular troops and 12 militia men, together with several families, evacuated the Fort. When about a mile on its march, Captain Heald observed that the Indians were preparing for an attack, and made dispositions for defence. A short conflict ensued, in which about one half of the garrison, and some women and children, were killed, when Captain Heald surrendered. The Fort was burnt by the Indians the next morning, and the prisoners were distributed among the bands.

The most distinguished victim of this short and sanguinary action, was Captain Wells. In his chagrin and despondency at the fate which the wilfulness and blindness of Captain Heald was bringing upon the whole retreating party, he had, according to the custom of the savages under such feelings, blackened his face, and was thus found among the slain. We have already alluded to his services and gallantry in General Wayne's campaign. His singular and eventful life, the energy and boldness of his character, entitle him to a passing notice. He was, while a child, captured by the Indians, and became the adopted son of the Little Turtle, the most eminent forest Warrior and Statesman of his time. In the defeats of Harmar and St. Clair he took a distinguished part, commanding in the latter action, three hundred young Warriors, who were posted immediately in front of the artillery, and caused such carnage among those who served it. He arranged his party behind logs and trees immediately under the knowl on which the guns were placed, and thence, almost uninjured, picked off the artillerists, until, it is said, their bodies were heaped up almost to the height of the pieces.

After this sanguinary affair, his forecast led him to anticipate the final ascendency of the whites, who would be roused, by these reverses, to such exertions, as must be successful with their preponderance of power; and he resolved to abandon the savages. His mode of announcing this determination, was in accordance with the simple and sententious habits of a forest life. He was traversing the woods in the morning with his adopted father, the Little Turtle, when, pointing to the heavens, he said, "When the sun reaches the meridian, I leave you for the whites; and whenever you meet me in battle, you must kill me, as I shall endeavor to do the same with you." The bonds of affection and respect which had bound these two singular and highly gifted men together, were not severed or weakened by this abrupt dereliction. Captain Wells soon after joined Wayne's army, and, by his intimacy with the wilderness, his perfect knowledge of the Indian haunts, habits, and modes of warfare, became an invaluable auxiliary to the Americans. He served faithfully, and fought bravely, through the campaign, and, at the close, when peace had restored amity between the Indians and the Whites, rejoined his foster father, the Little Turtle; and their friendship and connexion was broken only by the death of the latter. When his body was found among the slain at Chicago, the Indians are said to have drank his blood, from a superstitious belief that they should thus imbibe his warlike endowments, which had been considered by them as preeminent.

During the fall and winter succeeding these events, General Harrison had been collecting an army for the purpose of recovering the north-western frontier. Having advanced as far as Sandusky, he detached General Winchester, in advance, to the Maumee. Gen. Winchester sent forward a foraging party as far as the River Raisin, which reached that place on the 18th of January, 1813, and dislodged a body of Indians found there. The next day, General Winchester, with his main body, joined this advance, having a force of about one thousand men. He encamped on the left bank of the river; but although forewarned of the approach of a hostile party from Malden, it does not appear that he made any disposition of his troops to meet an emergency. On the 22d, early in the morning, his camp was attacked by the British and Indians. Portions of the line defended themselves with obstinacy and success, particularly the left, under Major Madison. Gen. Winchester himself, had taken lodgings on the opposite side of the river,* at some distance from the scene of action; and we have understood that he was captured before he joined his troops. Being without any general direction, the line, with the exception before mentioned, soon fell into confusion and gave way. A retreat was made across the river; but the savages, who anticipated such a movement, were in readiness there to meet the fugitives, and few escaped the slaughter. Major Madison continued to defend himself, until informed by General Winchester—then a prisoner—that his party had been surrendered. The obligation to submit to terms concluded under such circumstances, is

---

* Colonel Robert Navarre, at whose house General Winchester lodged, stated this fact.

more than doubtful; and it is probable that the gallant Major, deserted by all the rest of the line, saw no chance of final success, and surrendered as much from hard necessity as in obedience to the orders of his captive General.

The bloody scene which followed this disastrous morning, has given celebrity to the spot, far beyond the importance of this event. The massacre at the River Raisin will remain a sanguinary blot on the military fame of Britain, as long as her history shall be faithfully told. Most of the wounded were collected in one or two houses near the battle ground. General Winchester, whose situation enabled him to observe the conduct and disposition of the Anglo savages, felt an apprehension for the fate of these unfortunate sufferers, and frequently reminded Gen. Proctor of his solemn engagement to protect them. Whether his comparatively small number of regular troops could not control the cannibal ferocity of his allies, or whether he looked on their bloody orgies without opposition or remonstrance, may be left undetermined by the charity of history, as long as the proofs are at all questionable. There appears to be a dark shadow, suited to the blackness of the transaction, resting over it, and nothing perhaps is distinctly known, excepting the horrible result. Butchery and conflagration were at work through the night, and these unhappy victims who trusted to the mercy, or honor of the British character, were mostly, if not all, buried under a heap of smouldering ruins.

This series of events so unfortunate for the Americans and so triumphant for the British, filled the inhabitants of Michigan with despondency, and seemed to leave them in hopeless subjection to a foreign dominion. General Harrison's operations on the frontiers of Ohio, threw an occasional gleam on their dark fortunes. The signal triumph of Croghan at Sandusky, and some of the events at

Fort Meigs, showed that victory might still revisit the American arms. These operations, however, had no immediate influence on the condition of the Territory, until Perry's victory, on the 10th September, 1813, opened a passage over the lake for the American forces. This brilliant and important naval action, which was so instrumental in restoring Michigan to the Union, deserves particular notice, as an essential part of her history.

Commodore Perry's fleet had been built, under great disadvantages at Erie, Penn. The bar at the mouth of the harbour would not permit the vessels to pass out with their armament on board. For some time after the fleet was ready to sail, the British Commodore continued to hover off the harbour, well knowing it must either remain there inactive, or venture out with almost a certainty of defeat. During this blockade, Commodore Perry had no alternative but to ride at anchor at Erie. Fortunately, early in September, the enemy relaxed his vigilance, and withdrew to the upper end of the Lake. Commodore Perry seized the opportune moment to pass the bar, and fit his vessels for action. This triumph over the vigilance of the British was a presage of the still greater triumph that followed. On the 10th of September, at sunrise, while at anchor at Put-in-Bay, Commodore Perry discovered the enemy towards the head of the Lake. He immediately got under weigh, and with a favoring wind, brought him to action a few minutes before noon. His flag vessel, the Lawrence, was engaged with the whole force of the enemy for nearly two hours, before the wind permitted her consorts to join in close combat. She gallantly maintained the unequal fight, until all her rigging was cut to pieces, every gun rendered useless, and the greater part of her crew either killed or wounded. In this perilous condition, Commodore Perry adopted one of those bold and decisive resolutions, which often enable a great commander to convert an apparent defeat into a certain victory. He caused his boat to be lowered, and launched himself and his fortunes upon the bosom of the Lake, amid the showers of death that fell around him. Reaching the Niagara in safety, which was just coming into close action with a swelling breeze, he at once determined to break through the enemy's fleet, already somewhat crippled by the contest with the Lawrence. The Niagara had every rope and spar, every gun and man, untouched. She broke into the enemy's line in all the freshness of her might, and, ranging by the vessels in succession, and, pouring in her broadsides, compelled them one after the other to lower their flags in token of submission, until they all were "ours."* In achieving this decisive victory, the Niagara was assisted by the smaller vessels, which were brought into co-operation by Captain Elliot, who had volunteered in this service when Commodore Perry assumed command of his vessel. Not long after Commodore Perry boarded the Niagara, the Lawrence struck her colors. She was, however, but a fleeting trophy, for before she could be taken possession of, every British flag nad followed her humiliating example.

This consummate victory opened the Lake to General Harrison, who soon after crossed his army to the Canadian shore, and, in the course of a short campaign, which was brilliantly finished by the battle of the Moravian towns, drove the enemy from the north-western frontier. On the 29th September, 1813, Detroit was occupied by a detachment of his army. An armistice was concluded with the Indians on the 18th of October following; thus restoring tranquility and security to the Territory.

General Harrison soon after moved down with his main

---

*The sententious report of the gallant conqueror to General Harrison was, "We have met the enemy, and they are ours."

body to the Niagara frontier, and left General Cass in command at Detroit. No military movements took place during the winter following, excepting an incursion into the interior of the upper Province by Major Holmes, who was attacked near Stoney Creek, and maintained his ground with great bravery and success.

In the month of July 1814, an expedition was concerted for the purpose of recovering the island of Michilimackinac,* the only part of the Territory then remaining in the possession of the British. Lieutenant Colonel Croghan, who had so gallantly defended his post at Sandusky, had command of the land forces, and Commodore Sinclair of the fleet which transported them. The expedition reached the neighborhood of the island in safety; and had the attack been made without delay, it is probable that the post would have fallen. The chances of success were certainly diminished each moment the enemy had for the purpose of strengthening his defences and increasing his numbers. After hovering about the island a few days, the fleet sailed for the Straits of St. Mary, and sent a detachment against the British fur establishment on the island of St. Joseph's. This establishment was destroyed, as well as some public stores at another subordinate post. After fulfilling these minor objects of the expedition, the fleet returned to the neighborhood of the island of Michilimackinac. In the mean time, the British Commandant had diligently improved the time thus allowed to him, in strengthening his works, and calling

---

*The documents within my reach relative to the expedition against Michilimackinac, were imperfect and meagre. I could find neither Colonel Croghan's official account, nor Major Holmes' correspondence on the subject, and became dependent for the statement embodied in the address, on the account delivered to the Detroit Lyceum, before alluded to, and the recollection of a conversation with an officer who served in the expedition.

in such aid as the country afforded. Large bodies of Indians were collected, who became, under the circumstances with which the attack was made, the most efficient auxiliaries.

We have been informed by an officer connected with the expedition, that Colonel Croghan was desirous of being landed on the south-western side of the island, not far from the village. The shore was there unobstructed, the ascent to the high table land on which the Fort stands sufficiently practicable, and the grounds between that and the Fort generally free from coverts and undergrowth, which in all other parts of the island, afford such facilities for Indian warfare. Com. Sinclair is stated to have objected to the position which his vessels would be obliged to take for such a disembarkation, as it would expose them to the fire of the Fort. It was finally determined to land on the north-eastern side of the island, and the fleet was stationed accordingly. The island of Michilimackinac is about three miles in diameter, and was then mostly covered with a dense and almost impervious growth of small trees. This mass of vegetation was every where intersected by cart and bridal paths, which had the perplexity of a labyrinth. Here and there were patches of a few acres, which had been cleared and cultivated. Colonel Croghan, having landed his troops at a point nearly opposite to the Fort, had, of course, to traverse the whole width of the island amid these embarrassing obstacles. Every Indian, on such grounds, was more formidable than the best disciplined soldier. The numerous auxiliaries of this description, which the British commander had been able to collect during the absence of the fleet, were therefore superior to any equal reinforcement of regular troops he could have received. Had the landing been made on the other side of the island, near the village, these allies would have been rendered nearly useless, as their prudential mode of warfare is opposed to all exposure on open grounds.

The landing was easily effected, and the Americans suffered to advance into the labyrinths of the island, nearly to the centre, unobstructed, when, in approaching one of the clearings before alluded to, the enemy was found ready to receive them. A desultory firing began within the opening, very annoying and somewhat destructive to the Americans, when Major Holmes, a brave and accomplished officer, was directed to charge into the opposite thickets. While executing this order with great spirit, he fell mortally wounded. His party recoiled upon the main body, and Colonel Croghan soon retreated to his boats. All operations of the expedition of any importance, terminated with this failure, and the island of Michilimackinac remained in the hands of the British until the peace.

The interruption of the civil government of Michigan, which began with the capture of General Hull, was closed in October 9th, 1813, by the appointment of General Cass as Governor of the Territory; who soon after re-organised its institutions, and restored the operation of law and justice.

DISCOURSE,

DELIVERED BEFORE THE HISTORICAL SOCIETY OF MICHIGAN:

BY JOHN BIDDLE.

Preliminary Remarks—Some observations upon the early political condition and division of Michigan—The Territorial Limits of Michigan—Surveys of Public Lands, &c.—The Lead Mine country—Natural resources of Michigan, and her future Prospects—Ultimate disposal of the Public Lands considered—State Government.

DISCOURSE.

Gentlemen of the Historical Society:

The earlier period of the history of this country since it became known to Europeans, was presented to the Society by Governor Cass, in a discourse which must be yet fresh in the recollection of its auditors. This period embraces among the topics of its history, the discovery of unknown regions, and the stirring incidents of war and of perilous enterprise: and in reviewing the incidents of an age, which though comparatively recent, offers little in common with our own, the imagination is pleasingly exercised in realising circumstances and events, which the lapse of time places in a contrast so strong with those which are passing before us. These considerations render the portion of time I have referred to, the most interesting for an occasion like the present, and a narrative of its events could not but acquire fresh interest in the hands of one, the productions of whose pen are characterised by enlarged views, a philosophical spirit, a warm fancy, and a striking felicity of diction. He sketched rapidly but distinctly the first visit of the European to our shores in the course of the adventurous prosecution of the fur trade by the French, the wars with the aborigines which occurred during the dominion of that people, the courage and perseverance of the early explorers of a boundless wilderness, and the self-devotion of the martyrs to a pious zeal for the conversion of the savage. Commemorating the triumph of the British arms over their rivals, and the consequent destruction of French power upon this continent, he brought to our notice the various incidents which present themselves from that time to the epoch when the jurisdiction of the United States was extended to the country we inhabit.

To Mr. Schoolcraft the Society is indebted for a summary of the history of the Indian tribes which tradition or present location associates with the great lakes and their tributaries, and for some highly interesting general views of the history, manners, institutions, character and destinies of that branch of the human family. The position of that gentleman, his studies, his travels, and his observant and philosophical mind render his observations on these subjects particularly instructive, and the Society feels a just pride in numbering such a contribution among its original papers.

At the last anniversary of the Society, Major Whiting, in a succinct and perspicuous narrative, brought down the history of public occurrences connected with our Territory, to a recent period, embracing in his review, the painfully interesting events and circumstances of the late war. In this paper we find an accuracy of research and clearness of judgment characteristic of its author.

There thus remains for consideration, a period brief in point of time, unmarked by striking incidents, and such as it presents, familiar to those who hear me. But though offering nothing to rouse the imagination or to excite our sensibility, it is the period which, characterised as it is by the silent progress of improvement, will be contemplated with most pleasure by an enlightened judgment. To scenes of war and sense of feebleness and dependence have succeeded perfect tranquillity, and a feeling of confidence and security. The peninsula of Michigan, whose interior within less than the short space of twenty years, was scarcely known in its topography or general character, to the few inhabitants who then skirted its eastern border, and was believed to be for the most part an uninhabitable morass, has become the residence of an industrious and moral people, enjoying a full share of all the blessings which Providence has coferred so bountifully upon the American people. The poetic vision of the bard has been already realized in a wilderness beyond that to which his imagination carried him in his fervid invocation of the genius of improvement.

> "Come bright improvement! on the car of time,
> And rule the spacious world from clime to clime;
> Thy handmaid arts shall every wild explore,
> Trace every wave and culture every shore—
> On Erie's banks where tigers steal along,
> And the dread Indian chaunts a dismal song,
> Where human fiends on midnight errands walk,
> And bathe in blood the murderous tomahawk,
> There shall the flocks on thymy pasture stray,
> And shepherds dance at summer's opening day;
> Each wandering genius of the lonely glen
> Shall start to view the glitt'ring haunts of men,
> And silent watch on woodland heights around,
> The village curfew as it tolls profound."

Neither of the gentlemen who preceded me have adverted particularly to the political history of the country. I will therefore ask the attention of the society to a few imperfect details in relation to the civil institutions under which our public affairs have been administered. Under the French and British dominion, the points occupied on the eastern boundary of what now constitutes the Territory of Michigan, were considered a part of New France or Canada. Detroit was known to the French as Fort Pontchartrain of the strait of lake Erie, and is so styled in the early grants of land in this neighborhood. The military commandants under both governments appear to have exercised a civil jurisdiction over the settlements surrounding their posts. What were their powers, if defined at all, and in what forms administered, I have met with no authority which explains. They were probably indefinite and exercised in a simple and summary manner. Where the necessity of protection was so strongly felt, it may be supposed that no disposition existed to scan very critically the acts of those by whom the military arm was wielded. These powers, however, seem to have been exercised with sufficient discretion, if we may judge from the impressions remaining among some of our older inhabitants.

When possession of the country was yielded to the United States, in the year 1796, the British garrisons at Detroit and Michilimackinac were replaced by detachments from the army of General Wayne, and we became a part of the northwestern Territory. That Territory was then in the first stage of the government, prescribed by the ordinance of 1787. Arthur St. Clair was its governor, who was, therefore, the first American Chief Magistrate under whom this country was placed. In the year 1798, the northwestern Territory assumed what was called the second grade of Territorial government. The county of Wayne, then co-extensive with the Territory of Michigan as afterwards established, sent one representative to the General Assembly of the northwestern Territory, held at Chillicothe, whose election probably gave the first occasion for the exercise of the right of suffrage in this country. In the year 1800, Indiana was established as a separate Territory, embracing all the country lying west of the present State of Ohio, and of an extension of the western line of that State due north, to the territorial limits of the United States. In the year 1802, the peninsula was annexed by the act of Congress, which authorised the formation of that part of the north-western Territory which now constitutes Ohio, into a State, to the Territory of Indiana.

In the year 1805 Michigan commenced its separate existence. That part of the Territory as now established, which lies east of a north and south line drawn through the middle of lake Michigan, was formed into a distinct government by an act of Congress passed in that year. The provisions of the ordinance of 1787 continued to regulate the form of government. That ordinance, attributed to a distinguished jurist of Massachusetts, is considered, by high authority, as reflecting great honor upon its author. It wisely provides for the establishment of those fundamental principles of law, which are regarded as the best securities of civil and religious liberty, and political equality, and is marked in its provisions and its tone, by prudence, discretion and humanity. The prohibition of slavery which it contains may have saved the country north-west of the Ohio from an incalculable evil. Under this constitution granted to the inhabitants of the country north-west of the Ohio, for as such it may be considered, from the fact that its most important provisions are declared irrevocable without their consent, the executive power was vested in a governor; the judicial, in three judges; and the legislative in both united. These officers were appointed by the general government; their legislative authority was restricted to the adoption of laws from the codes of the several States. This was the form of government provided until the Territory should contain 5,000 free white males of full age, and it then became optional with the people to choose a legislative body from among themselves, to be supported, however, at their own proper cost. The recent legislation of Congress has been of a more liberal character, as well in providing a legislature upon better principles, at the expense of the United States, as in the footing upon which it has placed the elective franchise and eligibility to office. Under the ordinance a freehold qualification was required, both on the part of the elector, and to render an individual eligible to the General Assembly, which was under certain circumstances provided for. It does not derogate, however, from the Congress of 1787, that more weight should then have been given to considerations of economy, or that greater caution should have been manifested, when our political system was in its infancy, in the extension of popular rights.

In 1818, upon the admission of Illinois into the Union, all the territory lying north of that State and of Indiana was annexed to Michigan.

From 1805, when the Territory was erected, to 1819, our political condition, was in every respect, that prescribed by the ordinance of 1787. By an act passed in the latter year, the Territory was authorised to elect a delegate to Congress. Under the ordinance, this privilege only accrued to a Territory when it should have entered upon the second grade of government, and the delegate was then to be chosen by the General Assembly. By the act referred to, this power was given directly to the people, and the right of suffrage was extended to all taxable citizens. In the year 1823, the form of the territorial government was essentially changed by an act of Congress, which abrogated the legislative powers of the governor and judges, and granted more enlarged ones to a council, to be composed of nine persons selected by the President of the United States, from eighteen chosen by the electors of the Territory. By this law, eligibility to office was made co-extensive with the right of suffrage, as established by the act of 1819. The limitation of the tenure of the judicial office to a term of four years, is another important feature of the act of 1823. In the year 1825, all county offices with the exception of those of a judicial character, or whose functions connect them with the administration of justice, were made elective; and the appointments which remained in the hands of the Executive were made subject to the approval of the Legislative Council. In 1827, the electors of the Territory were authorised to choose a number of persons corresponding with that at which the members of the Council was fixed, and their election made absolute. Such is the present form of our government; certainly a liberal one to be maintained at the expense of the parent State. The Legislative Council is empowered to enact all laws not inconsistent with the ordinance of 1787 : their acts, however, are subject to be annulled by Congress, and to the absolute veto of the Executive of the Territory.

The question as to what shall constitute the future State of Michigan, is one of great interest. Among the provisions of the ordinance of 1787, which are pronounced Articles of Compact between the United States and the people of the Territory north-west of the Ohio river, it is declared that the Territory shall be divided into not more than five nor less than three States. Three States having been already formed, what remains must according to that compact constitute two additional ones only. The geographical features of the country require, almost necessarily a very unequal division, and Michigan, when its institutions become permanent, must be limited to the peninsula, and perhaps the tract to the north of it, lying east of a line drawn through the centre of lake Michigan. These were the limits assigned to the Territory when it was established as a separate jurisdiction, and it is maintained upon authority entitled to great respect, that they cannot be encroached upon without a violation of our rights. The question of limits has on three occasions particularly called the attention of the public. The pretensions of Ohio to curtail our soil though kept up with pertinacity seem to rest upon nothing but her own will. With a territory already so ample and so fruitful, she is desirous of wresting from us that part of Miami bay and its coasts which lie within our limits. That she has no shadow of title has been unanswerably shown by the statement of the case by Governor Cass. If Congress possesses the right to gratify her ambition of territorial aggrandisement, the impolicy of increasing by such a concession the ultimate inequality of Michigan among the States of the west, and adding strength where it is least needed, can hardly fail in deciding against its exercise. The question which has been raised with Indiana, is of a very different character. By the act which authorised the framing of a constitution, the northern limits assigned to that State is a line ten miles north of the southern bend of lake Michigan. The object in view was probably to give Indiana a footing on that lake, and if this object had been attained without despoiling us of a valuable tract of country which we could illy spare, its justice or expediency would not have been so questionable. But the act has been done, and we can resist it only on the ground that Congress has done that which its previous acts had divested it of a right to do. The ordinance of the Congress of the Confederation, to which it is necessary so constantly to refer in treating of the history of the country north-west of the Ohio, divides the whole surface into three parts, each fronting south on that river, and extending north to the territorial limits of the United States. These divisions it declares shall form future states which it designates as the western, the middle, and the eastern, corresponding with Illinois, Indiana and Ohio. As these provisions occur in that part of the ordinance which are declared to be in the nature of a compact, unalterable, but by common consent, much caution was necessary in framing them; and a proviso is added to that which relates to boundaries, reserving to Congress the power so far to vary the arrangement therein prescribed, as at its discretion, to form one or two additional States in that part of the Territory lying north of a line drawn east and west, through the southerly extreme of lake Michigan. It has been contended by some, that if Congress exercises at all the authority retained by this proviso, of erecting one or two States in addition to the three expressly provided for, it must be done in exact conformity with the supposed sense of the proviso, by bounding them on the south by the precise latitude of the southern extemity of lake Michigan. It is upon this ground alone, I conceive, that the part of our Territory lying west of lake Michigan, and which never has had a separate political existence, calls in question the right of Congress to give its present limits to the State of Illinois. Whatever may be the technical aspect of the subject as a question of legal construction, to the mind of an unprofessional enquirer, this position appears untenable. The effect of the article in question, and its proviso, would seem to be to give to the three States for whose future existence it provides, an unqualified right to extend their northern boundaries to the parallel of lake Michigan, leaving the country to the north of that line, to be disposed of as might be thereafter determined, with the single qualification, that it should not form more than two States. There is nothing in the language used, which appears capable of being construed into a guarantee of the future rights of the communities whose contingent existence is adverted to. In regard to their limits, if Congress should exercise the power reserved, the phraseology used is extremely vague: they are to be established, it is said, in that part of the north-western Territory lying north of the line so frequently referred to.

The claim of right on the part of the peninsula of Michigan to resist the encroachment of Indiana rests on stronger grounds. In the act of 1805, by which the Territory was created, its limits are precisely fixed, and it is declared that the Territory thus bounded shall have all the rights, privileges and advantages granted by the ordinance, to the people north-west of the Ohio. One of the most important of these is the right, guaranteed to the several divisions of that Territory, of entering into the Union as each might attain a population of 60,000 free inhabitants. To curtail the limits to which this provision of the ordinance was made applicable by the act of 1805, has been justly viewed by high authority, as an undoubted violation of a vested right. A further demonstration towards narrowing the boundary, which Michigan as a matter of expediency as well as of justice, should be allowed to retain, has been made in a bill for establishing a new Territorial Government heretofore introduced into Congress. By this bill, with the alleged views of giving to the proposed territory the natural boundary of the straits of Mackinac and the river St. Mary's, that part of our original domain lying east of the artificial line extending north from the head of lake Michigan, was to be severed from us. This would involve a further violation of the act of 1805.

A brief recapitulation of the periods and circumstances of the extinction of the Indian title to our soil, and of the measures connected with its settlement, may not be wholly devoid of interest. If the Indian title to any portion of the country was extinguished by either of the goverments which preceded that of the United States, it is believed to have been only in the neighborhoods of their military posts, and to what extent this may have been done I am not informed. In the year 1785, at the treaty held at Fort M'Intosh, with the Wyandot, Delaware, Chippewa, and

Ottawa nations, a strip of land, beginning at the River Raisin and extending to lake St. Clair, with a depth of six miles from the strait, was reserved to the United States, as was also twelve miles square at Michilimackinac. In this treaty the phraseology is used of allotting boundaries to the Indians and reserving certain lands to the United States. The use of such language where the purpose was the extinction of Indian title is among the evidences of the unsettled notions in relation to Indian rights, which seem to have prevailed from the foundation of the government. In the treaty of Fort Harmar, of 1787, all the stipulations embraced by the former in regard to the Territory are repeated. Among the cessions made at the treaty of Greenville, in 1795, the strip of land before mentioned, which embraces Detroit, was again yielded to the United States, as also twelve miles square at the Miami rapids, the islands of Michilimackinac and Blois Blanc, and a tract six miles by three on the main to the north of the first named Island. All gifts or grants made to the French or British governments are, without specifying them, ceded to the United States. In 1804, a land office was established at Detroit; but as at that period the Indian title to the soil was very partially extinguished, and no public lands had been surveyed, it probably had for its immediate object, an adjustment of the land titles of the Territory. Most of these were founded upon French grants, which were found, however, on examination, to be defective in some particulars, essential to their validity, under the regulations of that government. In 1807, an act of Congress was passed, granting to all individuals who were in possession of lands in the year 1796, when the country came under the jurisdiction of the United States, and who continued their occupancy to the date of the act, a confirmation of their claims to a certain extent. It is upon this law, and upon subsequent ones extending to the settlements on the upper lakes a like principle, with greater latitude as to dates, that most of the old land titles of the Territory rest.

In 1807, the Indian title to our soil was first extinguished to any considerable extent. In that year, Governor Hull held a treaty at Detroit, with the Pottawatamie, Ottawa, Chippewa, and Wyandot tribes, at which an extensive tract of country was ceded to the United States. The southern boundary of the cession was the Miami bay and river, and it embraced all the lands lying east of a line drawn due north from the mouth of the Au Glaize, a tributary of the Miami, till it should intersect the parallel of the outlet of lake Huron, and extending thence in a north-easterly direction to White Rock, on that lake. This cession embraced nearly one half of the peninsula from its southern limit to the foot of lake Huron; the line running due north from the mouth of the Au Glaize corresponding with what is now established as the principal meridian in reference to the surveys of the public lands. From 1807 to 1819, the Indian boundaries remained unchanged; in that year a treaty was made with the Chippewas of Sagana, by which their title to a considerable tract of country was extinguished. The cession then made, begins at a point nearly west from Detroit, in the line before mentioned, as being now known under the designation of the principal meridian; thence it extends west sixty miles, thence to the head of Thunder Bay river, and with the course of that river to lake Huron. This is the present boundary on the east side of the peninsula. Without entering into details which might prove fatiguing, it may be stated in conclusion of this part of my subject, that at the treaty held with the Ottawas, Chippewas and Pottawatamies at Chicago, in 1821, the country lying west of the cession of 1807 and 1819, and extending from our southern boundary to the Grand river and its most northerly source, was acquired by the United States. A glance at the map will show that on the western side of the peninsula, a considerable extent of country is still subject to the Indian title, embracing a section of some magnitude which is known to be valuable.

The first surveys of public lands in this Territory were made in the year 1816 or 1817, and in 1818 the country was laid open to settlement, by a portion of it being offered for sale under the authority of the government of the United States. This is the most important era in the history of Michigan, and from it may be dated the commencement of her march in the career of improvement. The antiquity of Detroit and the neighboring settlement, has been sometimes alluded to, in unfavorable contrast with the progress they have hitherto made. It is true, that Detroit was occupied at an early period as the site of a post, from which the fur-trade might be conveniently prosecuted; and so at a date still earlier, were Michilimackinac, Green Bay, and some yet more remote points, which have become again incorporated with the surrounding wilderness. But until the period last mentioned, there could be no immigration of agriculturalists to a country where lands were not to be procured, and the labor of these must lay the foundation of all extensive communities. Before that time, indeed, in view of our remote position, an attempt to extend hither the tide immigration, would have been, perhaps, premature and unsuccessful; as it might have proved even then, but for the revolution in the commercial prospects of the country bounding on the great lakes, effected by the accomplishment of that great enterprise, the construction of the Erie and Hudson Canal. As an American community founding its prosperity upon the permanent resources of its own industry, Michigan may date its origin from the year 1818; and if the original forest had then covered the shores of the Detroit river, there are grounds, at least plausible, for the supposition, that they might at this moment have exhibited a higher degree of improvement than that which we now witness.

By an act of Congress of the 6th of May 1812, providing bounty lands for the soldiers of the war then impending, two millions of acres were directed to be surveyed for that purpose in this Territory. This provision of the act referred to, was repealed in 1816, and the same quantity directed to be surveyed in Illinois and Arkansas, in addition to that already required to be laid off in those districts, for a like purpose. In connexion with the present estimation in which the lands of Michigan are held, it appears not a little remarkable, that this change was made in consequence of the very unfavorable representation of the country given by the surveyors sent to mark out these bounty lands. It has been suspected that these representations were made from some sinister motive. The suspicion is probably unjust; for besides that no inducement to misrepresentation suggests itself, it is undoubtedly true, that a great part of the soil of this peninsula has a most unpromising appearance. The larger portion of it presents a high and undulating surface, fashioned evidently by the action of water; it is thinly timbered with oak, to which the ravages of annual fires give an appearance the reverse of thrifty. There is upon these lands, generally no covering of earth formed by the decomposition of vegetable matter. Experience has shewn, however that they possess a principle of durable and improving fertility, due probably to the presence of lime in the composition of the soil. There are also occasionally found tracts of some extent, level, damp, and overspread by an immense growth of timber, which in a state of nature seem uninviting to the settler, if not wholly unfit for cultivation.

Such soils assume a new aspect under the hands of industry, and what was mistaken for a morass, waves with grain, or is converted into a luxuriant meadow. It is a fortunate circumstance for this Territory that no part of the military bounty lands were surveyed within its limits, as they have elsewhere been found, I believe, to embarrass rather than promote the settlement of the country of their location. Since the commencement of the surveys of the public lands they have been rapidly prosecuted. According to an estimate which I have made, the quantity that has now been surveyed amounts to about ten millions of acres; of which somewhat less than one million has been sold.

There are several points within the limits of our Territory, where small settlements have existed from an early period; besides Detroit there is Michilimackinac, the settlement on the St. Mary's river, that on the Fox river of Green Bay, and at Prairie-du-Chien. There was a military post on the river St. Clair under the French and British domination, but whether the present settlement on that river dates from that period I am not informed. In regard to all these places, interesting facts might probably be gleaned by a careful enquirer; but I have to regret that neither time nor opportunity has been afforded me for such enquiries. In regard to Detroit I will venture to add a few words to what has been said by the gentlemen who preceded me in relation to its peculiar history. The old town of Detroit occupied a site below or west of the centre of the present town: it was built entirely of wood, the streets were extremely narrow, space being probably economised to diminish the circuit of the stockade by which it was secured. In 1805, the town was entirely consumed by fire. Shortly after this catastrophe, an act of Congress was passed, directing the governor and judges, then exercising legislative powers, to lay out a new town, including the site of the one destroyed, and ten thousand acres of adjacent land. The act directs that a lot should be granted to every owner or occupant of a house in the old town, and the proceeds of the remainder applied to the erection of a Court house and Jail. It is from this fund thus accruing that the present public buildings have been erected in this city. The trust arising under the act is not yet, I believe, closed. The destruction of the old town is so far fortunate that it led to the adoption of a plan better adapted to a city, such as Detroit is probably destined to become; though the powers of the governor and judges in this respect might have been more judiciously exercised.

The country now forming a part of Michigan, known as the lead mines of the Upper Mississippi, is a most interesting region. The mineral country is intersected by the parallel of 42 1-2 degrees of latitude, which is established by law as the northern boundary of Illinois; but the largest and most productive portion of it, lies north of that line, and consequently, within the limits of our Territory. It is a district elevated and salubrious, with a surface beautifully varied by graceful undulations, covered with a luxuriant herbage, and abounds in streams of the purest water. Insulated conical hills, which are called mounds, give a peculiar character to the landscape, and serve as guides in traversing a country which in its state of nature, presents no obstacle to the progress of the traveller. The soil is eminently fertile, and its mineral wealth inexhaustible. Though the groves of trees scattered at intervals, are sufficiently numerous to relieve the eye, and to add to the picturesque beauty of the scenery, the want of wood in sufficient abundance for all useful purposes, must somewhat retard the settlement of this region, otherwise so inviting to the emigrant, and capable of maintaining a dense population. In the year 1804, the Sac and Fox Indians made a large cession of land to the United States, including an extensive district of the country above refered to. In 1816, by a treaty entered into with the Ottawas, Chippewas, and Pottawatamies, the United States relinquished to these tribes all that part of the cession made by the Sacs and Foxes, lying north of the southern bend of lake Michigan, and embracing the mineral country. There was reserved from this relinquishment only five leagues square, to be located by the President of the United States on and near the Mississippi and Ouisconsin rivers. These reservations were located on Fever river, and upon them not many years since, the manufacture of lead was commenced. This increased with great rapidity, and in 1829, the quantity manufactured, exceeded fourteen millions of pounds. At this period, the price of the article fell below the cost of production, under the disadvantageous circumstances in which the manufacturers were placed, obtaining as they were obliged to do, all their supplies from a distance. Discouragement consequently ensued, and the business was abandoned by many who had engaged in it. In the year 1829, a treaty was concluded at Prairie-du-Chien, with the Winnebago, Chippewa, Ottawa, and Pottawatamie tribes, by which, most of the land lying between the southern bend of Lake Michigan and the Fox and Ouisconsin rivers, embracing the whole country known to be rich in the mineral of lead, was ceded to the United States. When the measures now in operation, preparatory to the sale of these lands are completed, the agriculturalist will place himself by the side of the manufacturer, and the unequalled facilities which the country possesses for the manufacture of lead, will enable it to maintain a successful competition in that article, in the markets of the world.

——The length of the peninsula of Michigan, may be estimated at 280 miles, and its average breadth at 150. This gives it a superficies of upward of 40,000 square miles, and it will consequently hold a respectable rank in point of territory, among the States of the larger class. The country north of a line intersecting it near the centre, about the parallel of Sagana Bay is but little known, and is unfavorably represented. How far these representations may be relied on, the misapprehensions which formerly existed in relation to the whole interior, may lead us to doubt. But it is not improbable that much of the district in question, is of a very uninviting character, the soil being marshy, interspersed with sand ridges, and the climate severe. That part of the country lying south of the line before mentioned, has been explored, and for the most part surveyed, and is capable of sustaining a dense population. There are no mountains or barren hills, no extensive or irreclaimable marshes. Under the most unfavorable views, it may be assumed that the peninsula of Michigan will form a State respectable in point of population and resources; more especially when we advert to the characterestic feature of its geogrophy, the great extent of its coasts, so favorable to commerce and the formation of populous towns. While our own commercial exchanges are increasing with the development of our resources, the Upper Mississsippi will at no distant period, be connected with Lake Michigan by a canal or rail-road, the importance of the Upper Lakes as a channel of commerce will be greatly increased, and an extensive navigating interest will spring up in Michigan. Great facilities too, are known to exist for the extension of artificial navigation into the interior of the peninsula, and the general face of the country is highly favorable to the now favorite system of rail-roads. Our rivers are not extensively navigable, but though without falls, yet descending on either side upon inclined planes to the great Lakes, they furnish abundant water power for manufacturing purposes. Few minerals have been discovered in Eastern Michigan, nor does its general geological structure, I believe, favor an expectation, that it will prove rich in such productions. The existence, however, of iron ore within its limits, has been ascertained, and there are strong indications of mineral coal. It is said too, that gypsum is found upon some parts of the Grand river. This mineral, deemed so important in agriculture where its value is understood, abounds in the islands near Michilimackinac.

In adverting to the future advantages of Michigan, the liberal provision in lands for the advancement of education, which the General Government has made for us, in common with the other communities which have grown up under its parental care, should not be overlooked. This fund, carefully husbanded and judiciously administered, would seem to afford a most valuable resource in aid of a system for disseminating that general information, which does not every where receive, in practice, the attention due to its admitted importance to morals as well as to the maintenance of our political institutions. Our population, however, will be mainly derived from that stock of the American people, to which any reproach of neglect of the important interest of education is least applicable. The great predominance of the descendants of the New England race among the future inhabitants of Michigan, besides the guarantee that it affords, that intelligence and enterprise will not be wanting among them, will be attended with the further advantage that our population will be essentially homogeneous in its character; an advantage which will not be regarded lightly by those who have witnessed the difficulty of accomplishing an united action for objects of common interest, in some of the States of our Union, where the population, deriving their origin from various sources, from a discordant mass which it will require ages to amalgamate.

The question in regard to the ultimate disposal of the public lands, which has recently occupied much attention, is too deeply interesting to Michigan, to be considered foreign to my subject. It has been proposed, 1st, to cede them to the States in which they lie, for a pecuniary consideration to be paid to the other States—2d, to reduce the price, continuing the present system of sales, and receiving the proceeds as heretofore into the Treasury, as a part of the general revenue; and 3dly, to continue the present price and the same system of sales, and after paying in the first instance, to the States in which the lands lie, ten per cent, in addition to what is now allowed by law upon the amount received for lands sold within their limits respectively, to distribute the remainder among the other States, for certain specified purposes. Each of these projects proceeds from a source entitled to great respect. In regard to the first mentioned plan, it has been ably, and it appears to me, conclusively argued, that to dispose of them for a fair equivalent, might produce great embarrassment to the purchasing States, and would establish an invidious and dangerous relation of indefinite continuance, between the debtor and creditor States, besides being liable to other and very serious evils. On the other hand, to alienate the great public domain for a merely nominal consideration, would be an act of injustice to the older States, as well as a violation of the conditions upon which a large portion of it was ceded to the General government. The reduction of the price has been urged upon the grounds, that it is both politic and humane to give every facility to the acquisition of a freehold by the poorer classes of society; and, reviewing the payments for the public lands in the light of a tax, it is contended that this tax ought to be diminished with the reduction of the financial wants of the government. An argument founded upon the assumption that money voluntarily paid for an equivalent in land, is to be regarded as a tax, in the ordinary acceptation of the term, seems too strained to be entitled to much weight. The other branch of the argument in favor of reduction, has been answered by the assertion which seems well founded, that lands at the present price can be obtained by every industrious man with the degree of exertion necessary to teach him to appreciate the acquisition; and that in no point of view is it expedient to add further stimulus to the spreading of our population, or the diversion of a larger portion of labor into the channel of agriculture. It is further contended, that a reduction of the price of the public lands would seriously affect the value of the property of those whom the government is under every obligation to protect. The subject is not without difficulty in all its aspects; but the plan that proposes to leave untouched a system, of the excellence of which the evidence is so abundant, and after paying to each of the new States, 15 per cent upon the amount of sales within its limits, to distribute the balance among the other States for objects of the highest importance would seem, waiving the constitutional subtleties that have been applied to the question, judicious and liberal.

It has been contended, and I believe the doctrine has the sanction of the legislature of one or more of the Western States, that, on the admission of these States respectively into the Union, they became entitled of right to the public lands situated within their limits. The claim is founded, I believe, upon the assumption, that the right of soil to the unappropriated lands within the limits of its jurisdiction is an attribute of sovereignty. There is a clause too, in the ordinance of 1787, which provides that the States thereafter to be formed, shall be admitted into the confederacy upon an equal footing in all respects whatever with the original states; and it is argued, in regard to the new states to which the ordinance had been applicable, that this stipulated equality is not conceded unless the principle I have mentioned be recognised. It is held by those who entertain such views, that the condition attached to the admission of the new states, by which they are bound, not to interfere with the primary disposition of the soil by Congress, and by which lands, the property of the United States, are exempted from taxation, was imposed upon them in derogation of their rights. Upon this principle it has been suggested that if Michigan waits until her numbers amount to 60,000 (which the States heretofore organised have not done) before seeking admission into the Union, she may demand it as a right to enter into the confederacy untrammelled with any conditions. To sustain this doctrine it must be assumed that the act of 1805, establishing this Territory, definitely fixed the boundaries of the future State ; for if these are subject to change, we can have no positive right growing out of the number of inhabitants within any given limits. That we have vested rights with regard to Territorial limits under the act of 1805, I have before expressed a conviction ; though Congress in establishing the present boundaries of Indiana, virtually denies it. But, whatever be the merits of this question, the claim to right of soil to which I have adverted, rests upon a principle which whether well or ill founded, is too abstract and technical to stand in opposition to justice and to the conditions attached by Virginia to the cession of the North West Territory to the United States, and will probably never be acquiesced in. The legislation of Congress in regard to the public lands has been wise, liberal and paternal : the people of the flourishing communities which have grown up under it generally entertain sentiments in correspondence with its spirit ; and it is not probable that they can be induced by unscrupulous politicians eager to recommend themselves by an extravagant zeal for local interests, to offer to their fellow citizens the option of abandoning their interest in a common fund, or of submitting to a much worse alternative.

We are now on the eve of an important era in the history of our Territory, as its admission into the Union cannot be much longer deferred. If any difference of opinion now exists in relation to the expediency of immediate action upon this subject, the rapid advance of population must soon produce an unanimity of sentiment. Under the census of 1830, the peninsular counties of the Territory contained a population of about 28,000 souls. As the enumeration was made in the early part of the year, the number had no doubt risen to 30,000 before its close. To these we may probably add, without exaggeration, 10,000 for the increase during the year 1831. For the present year the accession from abroad will be considerably less, but, if measures were at once taken to obtain admission into the Union, there can be little doubt that before they could be consummated, our population would approach to, if it did not reach the number of 60,000. The Territory is certainly not laboring under any political disadvantages, which should urge the premature adoption of the important measure referred to. Heavy taxation, fiscal embarrassment, and the miserable financial expedients to which some of the new States have resorted, are greatly to be deprecated; but the time seems to have arrived, when we may without imprudence, indulge the natural desire for self-government.

Such are the few desultory facts and considerations connected with the country we inhabit, which I have to present to the Society; and I feel very sensibly, that I require all the indulgence which I am entitled to claim at your hands. In consenting to trespass upon your attention, I was influenced by a desire to manifest the interest felt in the purposes which the association has in view, rather than by an expectation of being able to offer it a contribution worthy of its acceptance. The little leisure I have had at command, since the duty of addressing the Society at its present anniversary was unexpectedly assigned to me, has precluded research, and, with the exception of a few dates supplied by an authority within immediate reach, thrown me almost exclusively upon such materials as memory could furnish. But I may be permitted to add, that it is only in comparison with the utter darkness which covers almost the whole face of the great West of America, that the annals of our own immediate district can be said to possess a degree of interest and copiousness. It has been remarked that while other nations dwell upon the past, Americans point proudly to the future. The observation is more particularly applicable to that region of our country, of which we form a part. While we exult, however, that the patriot and philanthropist can look with so much complacency on the future; that it presents such brilliant images to the speculative mind, we may be allowed to feel that our country is wanting in a great source of interest, and of pleasing sentiment, from the comparative absence of historical associations and monuments of past ages. Science has discredited the idea that ours is a new world in any other sense than the recency of its discovery by Europeans. Before the light of civilization had dawned where it has since shone with most brilliancy, the Indian probably launched his canoe upon our waters, and erected his frail wigwam upon our shores, as he did in the age which immediately preceded us. Yet, within the wide borders of this great empire, under various climates, in every variety of geographical position, he has not advanced one step beyond the rudest barbarism. When he leaves the soil to be succeeded by the descendant of the European, it seems fresh from the hands of nature. In the absence of all other memorials of the previous existence there of the human race, the occasional occurrence of inconsiderable and scattered mounds, owing their origin in fact, to the rudest mode of sepulture of the dead, has attracted curiosity and speculation.

In speaking thus I am not unmindful that there exists in the valley of the Ohio, and perhaps elsewhere, ramparts of earth which have been construed into evidence that the races of savages known to us have been in a more civilized condition, or that they were preceded by a people who had made some advance in the mechanic arts. But the imagination has been allowed to indulge in visions of the kind upon foundations so slight, as to justify incredulity in the sufficiency of the appearances referred to, to warrant the inference deduced from them. If our portion of this continent had ever been the residence of a civilized people, the fact would be attested by less equivocal testimony. In our climate the turf with which nature would envelope the ruins of the habitations of departed civilization, would form monuments of their existence that time could scarcely obliterate. Even the slight impressions left upon the surface of the ground by their rude tillage, may be sometimes observed long after the tribes to which they must be attributed, have retired and perhaps become extinct. Yet we traverse interminable forests and boundless plains without discovering the slightest indications that the soil has ever been disturbed by the hand of man. To what era then can we refer the existence of any thing but barbarism in this country, before it became known to Europeans?

NATURAL HISTORY.

THE FOLLOWING EXTRACTS RELATIVE TO THE NATURAL HISTORY OF MICHIGAN, ARE TAKEN FROM A LECTURE DELIVERED BEFORE THE DETROIT LYCEUM,

BY HENRY R. SCHOOLCRAFT.

There are not wanting in the wide-spread and beautiful regions which we inhabit, evidences to show that the great masters of European schools, however acute and learned, drew their conclusions from limited districts. And that nature, in the gigantic outlines which she has presented, in the area comprehended under the general term of the Mississippi Valley, and particularly, along the margins of the upper lakes, has not uniformly presented the same strata in the same relative position. We live, however, in a country, in which the industry of man has penetrated but little below the surface. The boring undertaken by the Hydraulic Company in this City, which was extended to the depth of 260 feet, did not penetrate into any primitive strata and did not result in the expected supply of water.

The work was commenced near the site of Fort Shelby, on the second rise of ground. Ten feet of alluvial earth was first passed through. Next a stratum of tenacious marly clay, with veins of quick sand—one hundred and fifteen feet. Two feet of beach sand with pebblestones succeeded, and the rock was then struck. It consisted of a stratum of geodiferous lime rock, sixty feet in depth. The auger then penetrated sixty-five feet into lias, in the course of which it fell into a cavity two and one-fourth inches in depth. A stratum of carbonate of lime, impregnated with salt, in a rather friable and yielding form, succeeded. This appears to be a subordinate bed in the lias, for the latter was again found below it, and the boring continued eight feet.

Mr Lucius Lyon who has communicated these facts, with specimens of the borings, to the Historical Society, is of opinion that the strata have a dip of fifteen minutes S. E.—an opinion rendered probable by the appearances of the geodiferous lime rock on the surface of the earth on the river Huron, about fifty miles N. W. The same stratum exists on Grosse Isle and Stony Island, and at Monguagon, near the mouth of the Detroit river, where the rock is characterized by cavities lined with crystals of sulphate of strontian.

The succession of strata across the peninsula, appears to be geodiferous lime rock, ferriferous, or brown sand rock, and *calcaire grossier*, the latter of which appears in a pure, white, friable mass in Jackson county. The heavy deposite of soil renders it difficult to make geological observations and the subject itself, has received but little attention.

An elongated area of elevated table land, separates the intesecting rivers of the peninsula. This assumes, more distinctly, the character of a ridge, as it is traced north, and appears to attain its greatest elevation in the Highlands of Sauble. At the foot of these Highlands, along the open shores of lake Huron, including the islands of Sagana bay and Thunder bay, there is an extensive formation of compact secondary limestone, having overlaying patches of a carbonaceous sedimentary limerock, replete with perfect organic remains. The Manatoulin chain, with its broken and denuded cliffs, is manifestly a residuary mass of the compact formation, and is mineralogically, a carbonate of lime of an excellent quality for economical purposes. This chain appears also, to have been overlaid by the carbonaceous limerock, and the locality yields casts and impressions of the articulated and shell animals. The island of Mackinac is based on the compact limestone, supporting a thick deposite of the sedimentary rock.

The primitive formation rises in the county of Chippewa, on the straits connecting Huron and Superior. But we shall only make use of this fact to remark, that it is not known to extend to the peninsula itself. The great size and number of the primitive boulders accumulated on the shores of lake Huron, between Fort Gratiot and Point aux Barques, renders it probable, however, that the primitive formation extends beneath this shore, and that it is near the surface, or perhaps rises through it, at some spot not visited, or back from the shore.

From the present state of our information, however, we must consider the entire peninsula as made up of secondary formations. They are obscured with deep deposites of soil, as at the city of Detroit, and it is chiefly, where the streams of the interior have cut through these deposites, that the rock flooring of the Territory becomes visible.

The positive elevation of the table land, between the two lakes, is not known. It has been estimated at three hundred feet. It is sufficient at any rate, to permit the streams to pass off in lively and healthful channels. And these channels present a sufficient descent, in the principal streams, to permit the erection of water mills. The aspect of the country itself, is of a highly picturesque character, and the number of small lakes of pure water which abound upon the uplands, together with the proportion which forests bear, to what are called *prairies*, secure for it the principal advantages, which are necessary to the growth and prosperity of an agricultural population. There is one character in its soil, which, if it has been observed in other portions of the Mississippi and Ohio uplands, has not been brought to our notice. Those portions of its table lands, which contain the fewest forest trees, and present a yellowish or reddish hue, impressing the passing traveller with the idea of sterility, undergo a chemical action, on being turned up by the plough, which changes the color of the soil to a qualified black, and the soil itself is found, in a high degree productive.

Our notices of the mineralogy of the country, must necessarily be brief. And in the rapid survey which it is proposed to take, we feel that expectation will be best satisfied, by directing the attention to that which is *useful*, rather than to that which is *merely curious*. This object will probably be further attained by confining the notices to the section of country, which it is expected, will remain in perpetuity, an integral portion of Michigan.

The lead mines of Iowa and Galena, which have yielded upwards of forty millions of pounds in seven years,* and the strong indications of copper mines, afforded by what is known of the southern coast of lake Superior, belong to the consideration of a region of country, in itself of immense extent,—which has been but imperfectly explored, and which presents *geological* as well as *mineralogical* features, in some respects peculiar, at least distinct and separate from the agricultural plains of the Peninsula. And no adequate notice could be taken of the mineralogy of that interesting section of our western country, without exceeding the limits of a single lecture.

It has been stated that the geological structure of the Peninsula is referable to the series of *floetz*, or horizontal

---

*40,088,960. Report of ord. off. 1830.

rocks. It is not only referable to this class of strata, but they assume in general, that sedimentary and noncrystalline character, which are deemed favorable to the existence of salt—of coal, and of gypsum—three products of value in the Territory at this time, but which will probably become more in request, as the increase of population produces an increase of consumption. Brine springs are known to exist in Washtenaw county; on the head of the Cheboigan river, and in some other places. It is now supposed that saline waters proceed from the dilution of rock salt in the lower strata, and that the waters are more or less strongly impregnated in proportion to the distance of these saline repositories, and other circumstances. Gypsum is found upon the cluster of St Martin's islands, in lake Huron; upon the island called by the natives, Neekiminis, and on the sources of Grand river.

Carbon and bitumen, under the combinations which these bodies assume in the bituminous state, are found in the wilderness parts of the counties of Sagana and Lapeer, and slaty coal and naptha, along the borders of Lake Michigan. We have picked up, along the margin of this lake, masses of mineral coal, fretted into the shape of spheroidal pebbles, which on breaking, exhibited a slaty and conchoidal structure, and were readily ignited, with a bituminous odour and flame. Nearly similar, in local position, we have discovered masses of a dark colored and sedimentary limestone, containing cavities filled with naptha, so hardened, where exposed to the air, as to exhibit the appearance of asphaltum, or of dried tar.

The structure of the Peninsula has been called *secondary,* without any reference to those foreign boulders of granite and trap rocks which are scattered over the soil, and load the shores of the larger lakes and rivers as if to remind the observer, that powers had formally been in operation, which are in operation no longer. One of the most noted of these fragmentary rocks, is the White Rock, so called. This is an object which has been known, since the first settlement of the country by the French. It is a vast mass of "transition" limestone, lying in, and reaching above the waters of Lake Huron, along that part of the coast, which is designated "Sanilac" upon the maps. Not far from it, in the margin of the lake, a mass of native silver was discovered in 1824, but this also, appeared to be extraneous, and no part of a contiguous body. The alum slate and the chalcedony of Sagana Bay, the sulphate of strontian of Grossé Isle, the calcareous spar of river Raisin, the grains of sand and vegetable substances invested with iron pyrites of Grand river, and the calcareous incrustations of the river St. Joseph, may be noticed among the objects of mineralogical interest.

* * * * * *

Whatever races of animals, either carnivorous or graminivorous, may have inhabited the country in former times, as may be inferred from their fossil remains, the white bear appears to be the strongest and most ferocious among the existing species. A bear in all his characters, he is more exclusively carnivorous than others of the species, and appears to possess, among quadrupeds, that superiority which the kind of eagle locally called *canieu*, holds among birds. At his approach all other animals retire. He is endowed with strength to tear the rib from the Bison at one stroke of the paw. His usual method of killing this animal is, however, to clasp his paws around its neck and dislocate the spine. The fear of him is not only imprinted upon the brute creation, but the Indian tribes, who inhabit that portion of our territory, where this animal is still found, regard him as their most formidable enemy. To overcome and kill him is not only a mark of personal distinction, but it is a distinction which is remembered through life, and attends a hunter to his grave. The skin of the slain enemy is exibited in triumph; the claws are worn as ornaments around the neck, and the tusks are regarded as endowed with medicinal properties, among a people who have not separated the belief in the efficacy of magic, from a belief in the efficacy of medicine.

The *Carcajou* is an animal of the same species, and the same region. Although quite inferior in point of size and strength, this animal appears to be endowed with a gluttonous appetite, and a propensity to destroy whatever is the result of human labor, which is very remarkable. He will pull down and deface temporary structures, and gorge himself on scaffolded meat. He will dig up the provisions left *en cache*, as it is termed, and when disappointed, it would seem, in the expectation of food, will commit wanton depredations on other property. He has been known to knaw in pieces a gunstock and powder horn, which it would seem, could not be done with the expectation of finding food within them. Unlike the white bear in its exterior, which is black, it is also unlike it in fleeing before the face of man. Its voraciousness is the voraciousness of stealth, and its depredations are committed when there is none to molest it. This shy and vicious animal is the *ursus luscus* of the systems, and the wolverine of the dealers in fur.

The *Cariboo* is the rein-deer of North America. This animal is confined to that portion of our Territory which embraces the borders of Lake Superior. It possesses most of the characters of the red deer, and its flesh is esteemed a very delicate venison. Its tongue has somewhat of the consistence of marrow, and when suitably prepared, and not injured by the pyroligneous acid of smoke, furnishes an article of epicurean delicacy. The hoof of this animal, like all the deer species, is split, but it is more thin, broad and delicate, and when placed on the ground, expands over a superfices which I have estimated to cover forty square inches. This lightness and expansion of the hoof enables it to travel on snow, when the snow is compacted or crusted. Its antlers are slightly palmated, and are re-produced, as far as is known, at the ordinary periods. Its food, in a climate of rigorous cold, where the soil is covered with snow more than half the year, consists of the bark of trees. Its lower front teeth are cutters. It is destitute of front teeth in the upper jaw.

The *Buffalo*, or what is more properly called the *Bison*, is not now found to inhabit east of the Mississippi. And in the extensive plains west of this stream, is receding fast towards the broken eminences of the Rocky mountains, where it will probably find a protection, at least from the presence of an agricultural population. Not half a century has past, since this animal existed in large herds, on the alluvions of Kentucky. And in periods, less remote, it was chased on the prairie lands of Illinois and Indiana. But ten years ago, it was known to inhabit the plains of the east banks of the Mississippi, above the Falls of St. Anthony. It is now never seen there. And its rapid recession, is a striking proof of the shortness of the period during which the larger native quadrupeds of a country, will abide in the face of advancing settlements. All attempts to domesticate the Bison, and to produce modifications of it, from the stock of the European cow, have heretofore failed. Its robes have constituted, and still constitute, an important item in our internal commerce. Its wool was manufactured into hats, socks, and a kind of heavy woollens, attempted to be substituted for stroads, in the colony founded by the Earl of Selkirk on Red river.

The *Musk-ox*, an animal not abundant where it is known

to exist, is not known to have ever been seen within our boundaries. The *Moose* is confined to the portions of country northwest of Lake Huron, where it is still relied on, by the Indian tribes, as among the means of their precarious subsistence. It is an animal quick of hearing and shy of approach, in consequence of which it is hunted with watchful assiduity. The Indians, who impute to medicine a mystical use, draw the figure of this, as of other animals, upon charts of bark or wood. And by applying their medicine to this visible sign, suppose a connexion to exist between it and the real animal. They thus affect to influence the animal, particularly during the performance of their medicine ceremonies and songs. In 1826, the traders of Fond du Lac had taken the pains to have the skin of an individual of this species stuffed and set up in the loft of a store room. The Indians of the post, who deemed this an improper use of the skin, remonstrated against it. They alleged that they could no longer kill the animal, whom they deemed thus degraded. And the traders were finally compelled to yield the point, and took down the offensive object.

In noticing the quadrupeds which are peculiar to our north-western borders, it may be said that the *Artic Fox* has been occasionally seen and killed there, during the winter season. This is one of the most beautiful of the lesser quadrupeds, possessing a coating of immaculate whiteness. The extreme point of its nose, and a few hairs within the ear are black, but the rest of the animal is covered with hair, interspersed with downy fibre, so entirely white, as to be, with difficulty, distinguished from the snow itself. Its tail is flowing, like that of the common fox, which it also resembles in general shape. Its nails are protected, like all animals of high northern latitudes, by a protrusion of woolly substance rather than hair.

The *Gopher*, is a small burrowing animal, which was not known to inhabit so far north, until 1820. It was found in the prairies of the Upper Mississippi, near St. Anthony's falls. This animal appears to subsist on roots, and to enable it to proceed in its subterranean search, nature has provided a duplicature of the cheek, extending as a sack inwardly. This sack is filled with earth by the paws, and inverted, and the contents discharged at the surface of the ground. When these sacks are extended outwardly, in the dried specimen, they protrude in a manner which gives it a very grotesque appearance. In this condition a prepared specimen was transmitted by Governor Cass to New York. And it may be mentioned as one of the results, which should put naturalists perpetually upon their guard against the admission of new species, that the animal was, at first, described and published, with these extraordinary appendant pouches, under the supposition that they occupied their natural position.

An animal of the mouse type has been found on the southern shores of Lake Superior, whose hinder legs are so much longer than its fore legs, as to give it, in this respect, a character analogous to that singular Australasian quadruped, the Kangaroo. And from its power of leaping, it has been locally called the *Jumping Mouse*. Very little is known of its habits.

A species of squirrel, having twelve or thirteen stripes, has been deemed peculiar, and described under the name of *sciurus tredeceum*. It inhabits the upper district of the Territory.

Our ornithology is of a character rich and varied, as well in those species inhabiting the land, as in those peculiar to the water. But it is a field in which but little has been done, either in the way of verifying known species, or bringing to light unknown. Being, in their nature, migratory, as well as gregarious, most of the species leave the country, particularly the northern portions of it, during the winter season. Of those which remain north of the latitude of 45 deg. the raven, the two varieties of partridge, and some of the smaller species of pica, or woodpecker, are the most prominent. The forests in those high latitudes are extremely solitary, and they would be still more so, were they not a temporary resort of some of the feathered tribes, from the still more northern latitudes of Canada, Hudson's Bay and the Artic circle. The white partridge, (*tetrao albus*) the great white owl, (*strix nyctea*) and the Canada jay, are thus brought within our limits. And each of these species has been killed on the Straits of St. Mary.

Winter in that latitude assumes its sternest character. And it must be difficult to form just conceptions of its polar aspect, by those who have been accustomed to the milder and modified climate of the peninsula. The great body of snow and ice prevents all vegetable exhalations from the earth for many months. The air is thus deprived of its extraneous qualities, and brought back to its original constitution of oxygen and nitrogen. The caloric, which passes through it, without entering into its composition, is readily withdrawn, and during the absence of the sun, the air attains its lowest point of temperature. The thermometer has there been known to stand at 33 deg. below zero, and it is frequently at 20 deg. Snow and ice are feeble reflectors of solar heat, and the influence of the sun when it is not intercepted by clouds, is counteracted by currents of wind from northerly points of the compass.

The abstraction of heat from the atmosphere renders the waters comparatively warm, and wherever there are falls or air holes in the body of investing ice, there is an evaporation, similar to that of a boiling pot. The columns of vapor ascend in a manner which is very striking, until the sun re-appears, to equalise, in some measure, the atmospheric temperature. The column of smoke from a chimney, during the early part of the morning, has a decidedly reddish, and not its ordinary hue. The air thus cooled, is breathed without difficulty. It appears to impart its oxygen to the lungs very freely; and to bodies not constitutionally diseased, the climate itself is eminently healthy. These are some of the characteristics of the winter climate north of lake Huron, where the existence of the oceanic mass of lake Superior, and the contiguity of the Hudson's Bay and artic ice-plains, produce a depression of temperature, which would by no means be inferred from the mere theory of latitudes.

It has already been remarked, that the birds and quadrupeds of that region are protected, in an unusual manner, by nature. All the quadrupeds, which are not amphibious, have an extra supply of protecting hair or fur. And those species of birds who are designed to abide in the country, are profusely covered with feathers, and feathery fibre, even down to, and around their claws. Yet I have known the Canada jay, which is a bird, having the property of rolling itself up, as it were, in its feathers, and presenting to the eye a globular mass, to freeze to death, at night, within my office. although this bird is capable of sustaining itself in the open atmosphere.

It will be inferred that those species of birds who come with the spring and retire with the autumn, constitute by far the greater proportion. Of the aquatic species, there are some kinds of duck, who appear, generally, to remain. They procure a subsistence by hovering about the falls and rapids, which are numerous at that altitude. And they are frequently seen at the falls to ride down the waves, and on flying out, at the bottom, to repeat the operation. On dissecting these ducks, small insects have been found, and these, with some scanty vegetable substances, appear to constitute their food. There are others, who come at an early period of the spring, and retire very late in the fall, or in the commencement of the winter, who appear to subsist upon fish.

The pelican, although a common summer bird on the upper Mississippi, extending quite to its sources, is not an inhabitant, and we think not a visitant, of the Great Lakes, the shores of which probably, are unfavorable to the peculiar mode of its capturing the small fish which serve as its food. The cormorant, or what the natives, with particular reference to its *mandible* and its *color*, denominate the crow-duck, (Kah-gah-gee-sheeb) is probably deterred by similar circumstances, from extending its migrations in this direction.

The species of vulture which is known under the name of turkey-buzzard, does not inhabit so far north. The *galliparo meleagris*, or wild turkey, pursues its food in the vast ranges of the new counties of the peninsula, and is still found in the vicinity of this city. It does not extend its summer migrations to the extremity of the peninsula, and has never been seen north of it.

During the winter of 1824, a small bird, of peculiar plumage, appeared in the forests at the foot of lake Superior. It was recognised by the natives, as one seldom or never seen so far south and east, but known to inhabit more northerly latitudes. They denominated it *paush-kan-di-mo*, a term in its general signification, coinciding very nearly with the Latin generic *fringilla*. Having obtained a specimen, we submitted it for examination at New-York and Philadelphia, where it was determined to be a new, or undescribed species of the grosbeck, and it was transferred to this family, under the name of *F. Vespertina*, or evening grosbeck, in allusion to the observed time of its singing.

Ichthyology has scarcely extended its researches into this

quarter. Yet it must be evident, upon a slight examination, that the northern waters present an interesting theatre of observation. The great chain of lakes, stretching across sixteen degrees of longitude, and embracing fourteen degrees of latitude, present in themselves an area, compared to which, the lakes of the old world are diminutive. But it is an area which nearly excludes those fishes who thrive best in warm and turbid waters, or attain their least perfection in those that are cold and transparent. And we attach more importance, in the distribution of species by nature, to these principles, than to any physical impossibility of communication between the lakes and south-western rivers. Some inquirers, more curious, perhaps, than wise, have attempted partially, a new distribution, but without the slightest evidences of success. The eel has, for instance, been taken from the foot of Niagara falls to the river above, and in a manner apparently, to ensure success to the experiment; yet nobody has observed that eels have become products to the lake waters; although such streams as the Tonewanta and the Maumee, would seem to be favorable to their re-production. And were there not something ungenial in the waters themselves, it appears difficult to conclude that such experiments would not meet with success. We have it on good authority, that eels have been occasionally taken in Chicago creek, an inlet of Lake Michigan, but they have not been found in Lake Michigan itself. Lamprey eels exist in the lakes. And we have observed the gar, a species common to the turbid waters of the lower Mississippi, and a species of the Amia, (Shig-wam-aig) heretofore found only in the rivers of Georgia. Both these varieties have been noticed in those expansions of the channel denominated lakes in the Straits of St. Mary.

But the most important of our lake fishes, considered in reference to its value in commerce, is the white fish. This fish is found to inhabit the lake waters, in the whole extent of the series, at least above Niagara Falls. It is more particularly taken in the Straits of Detroit and St. Clair, and in those of St. Mary's and Michilimackinac. And the quantity put up, during the last season, (1830) has been estimated at 8,000 barrels, valued at $40,000. It is not only found in our mediterranean lakes, but also, in the small lakes situated at the sources of the Mississippi, which have their outlets into that stream. It is thus diffused over the northern hemisphere, at least from the latitude of Pecá-ga-mah, the uppermost fall of the Mississippi, to the head waters of St. Croix and Chippewa rivers. But it has not been known to descend those rivers into the Mississippi; nor has an individual of the species been observed in the Mississippi, even where its waters are the clearest. No physical obstruction exists for their passage out of these tributary streams; and it is difficult to conceive any reason for this exclusive occupation of these upper waters, without referring to a law of nature, which has adapted their habits, both of migration and subsistence, particularly to these small lake waters. And it appears manifest, that with respect to these Mississippian lakes, the range of their migration must be very limited, and their winter abode confined.

REMARKS,

ON THE SUPPOSED TIDES, AND PERIODICAL RISE AND FALL OF THE NORTH AMERICAN LAKES.

BY HENRY WHITING.

In the article "on the supposed tides in the great North American Lakes," communicated by General H. A. S. Dearborn, (Vol. XVI. No. 1. April, 1829,) it is stated that Governor Cass had been requested to cause observations to be made, during his stay at Green Bay, on the changes of elevation in the waters at that place. In the year 1828 while there on public duties, he did so, during the course of more than six weeks. The following table is the result, presenting a series of observations of such extent and minuteness, as to determine as satisfactorily, perhaps, as the case admits, the character of the phenomenon in question. A cask, without heads, was fixed in the Fox river, just within its mouth, with a rod, graduated with inches, placed perpendicularly in the centre. The cask was perforated so as to admit the water freely, while the rod, at the same time, was protected from such fluctuations of the surface as the wind might cause.

Table of observations on the rise and fall of the Lake at Green Bay, made by Gov. Cass in 1828.

Day of the month	Time of the day.	Course of the wind.	Strength of the wind	Height of the water.
July 15, 1828.	9	N.	Moderate.	9
"	Noon.	"	"	8
"	4	"	"	5 1-2
"	7 1-2	"	"	11
16.	6 1-2	W.	Light.	10
"	8	"	"	10 1-2
"	1	"	"	6
"	4	"	"	6
"	7 1-2	"	"	6 1-2
17.	6	S. W.	"	6
"	8	"	"	8 1-4
"	Noon.	"	"	6
"	4	"	"	5 1-2
"	7 1-2	"	"	8
18.	6	"	"	1
"	8	"	"	4
"	Noon	"	Strong.	7
"	4	"	"	4
"	7 1-2	"	"	7
19,	6	W of S W	Light.	7
"	8	"	"	5
"	9	"	"	11
"	Noon.	"	"	5 1-2
"	4	"	"	7
"	7 1-2	"	"	6 1-2
20,	8	No wind	None.	6
"	Noon.	N. W.	Light.	8
"	4	"	"	10
"	7 1-2	"	"	5 1-2
21,	8	S. W.	"	9 1-2
"	2	"	"	10
"	4	"	"	
"	7 1-2	N.	Vil't storm	18
22,	7	S. W.	Light.	10
"	Noon.	"	"	0
"	4	"	"	14

Day of the month	Time of the Day	Course of the Wind.	Strength of the wind.	Height of the Water.
Au. 22,	7 1-2	S. W.	Light.	11
23,	8	"	Moderate.	3 1-2
"	Noon.	"	"	1 1-2
"	4	"	"	11 1-2
"	7 1-2	"	"	11
24,	8	N. E.	Light.	9
"	Noon.	"	"	8
"	4	"	"	14
"	7 1-2	"	"	10
25,	8	S. W.	Moderate.	5 1-2
"	Noon.	"	"	5 1-2
"	4	"	"	9 1-2
"	7 1-2	"	"	12 1-2
26,	8	"	Light.	11
"	Noon.	"	"	10
"	4	"	"	8 1-2
"	7 1-2	"	"	7
27,	8	W.	"	10 1-2
"	Noon.	"	"	6
"	4	"	"	2
"	7 1-2	"	"	12
28,	8	N.	Fresh.	4
"	Noon.	"	"	11
"	4	"	"	2
"	7 1-2	"	"	8 1-8
29,	8	S. W.	Light.	11
"	Noon.	"	"	6 1-2
"	4	"	"	4
"	7 1-2	"	"	8
30,	8	N. W.	"	9
"	Noon.	"	"	5
"	4	"	"	9
31,	8	S. W.	"	7
"	Noon.	"	"	7
"	4	"	"	8
"	7 1-2	"	"	7 1-2
Aug. 1,	8	N.	"	13
"	Noon.	"	"	9
"	4	"	"	7

Day of the Month.	Time of the day.	Course of the Wind.	Strength of the wind	Height of the Water.
Aug. 1,	7 1-2	N.	Light.	8
2,	8	N. E.	"	7
"	Noon.	"	"	11
"	4	"	"	1
"	7 1-2	"	"	11
3,	8	S. W.	"	4
"	Noon.	"	"	10
"	4	"	"	7
"	7 1-2	"	"	9
"	9	"	"	7
4,	8	N. W.	"	7
"	Noon.	"	"	8
"	4	"	"	12
"	7 1-2	"	"	5
5,	8	S. W.	"	6
"	Noon.	"	"	6 1-2
"	4	"	"	12
"	7½	"	"	7
6,	8	"	"	6
"	Noon.	"	"	9
"	4	"	"	8
"	7 1-2	"	"	10
7,	8	"	"	8
"	Noon.	"	"	6
"	7 1-2	"	"	9
8,	Noon.	N.	"	6
"	4	"	"	7
"	7 1-2	"	"	7
9,	8	S. W.	Strong.	2
"	Noon.	"	"	0
"	4	"	"	13
"	7 1-2	"	"	6
10,	8	N. E.	pretty fresh	13
"	Noon.	"	"	9
"	4	"	"	10
"	7 1-2	"	"	16
11,	8	"	Light.	10
"	Noon.	"	"	8
"	4	"	"	6

Day of the month.	Time of the day.	Course the wind.	Strength of the wind.	Height of the water.
Au. 11,	7 1-2	N. E.	Light.	7
12,	8	S. W.	"	8
"	Noon.	"	"	2
"	4	"	"	5
"	7 1-2	"	"	9
13,	8	"	"	10
"	Noon.	"	"	5
"	4	"	"	4 1-2
"	7 1-2	"	"	9
14,	8	"	Moderate.	4
"	Noon.	"	"	5
"	4	"	"	6
"	7 1-2	"	"	5
15,	8	N.	Fresh.	10
"	Noon.	"	"	6
"	4	"	"	3
"	7 1-2	"	"	4
16,	8	S. W.	Light.	6
"	Noon.	"	"	6
"	4	"	"	5
"	7 1-2	"	"	7
17,	8	N.	"	7
"	Noon.	"	"	3
"	4	"	"	11
"	7 1-2	"	"	7
18,	8	N. W.	"	4
"	Noon.	"	"	7
18,	4	"	"	10
"	7 1-2	"	"	5
19,	8	S.	Fresh.	4
"	Noon.	"	"	8
"	8	"	"	8
"	7 1-2	"	"	5
20,	8	S. W.	Light.	5
"	Noon.	"	"	7
"	4	"	"	11
"	7 1-2	"	"	8
21,	8	N.	"	6
"	Noon.	"	"	8

Day of the month.	Time of the day.	Course of the wind.	Strength of the wind.	Height of the water.
Au. 21,	4	N.	Light.	10
"	7 1-2	"	"	9
22,	8	No wind.	"	10
"	Noon.	"	"	7
"	4	"	"	11
"	7 1-2	"	"	14
23,	8	S. W.	"	8
"	Noon.	"	"	7
"	4	"	"	11
"	7 1-2	"	"	7
24,	8	"	Moderate.	8
"	Noon.	"	"	9
"	4	"	"	7
"	7 1-2	"	"	8
25,	8	"	Light.	10
"	Noon.	"	"	4
"	4	"	"	11
"	7 1-2	"	"	13
26,	8	Northerly.	"	12
"	Noon.	"	"	8
"	4	"	"	10
"	7 1-2	"	"	7
27,	8	"	"	12
"	Noon.	"	"	8
"	4	"	"	9
"	7 1-2	"	"	14
28,	8	"	"	12
29,	Noon.	"	"	13

An examination of the foregoing table will probably satisfy most minds, that planetary influence has little or nothing to do with the changes of elevation in the waters there noted. The oceanic tides, though somewhat modified in their height and recurrence by winds, and other terrestrial agents, are, nevertheless, so regular in their flux and reflux, as to show a constant and inseparable connexion with the movements of the moon and sun. We presume the only question here to be, whether the apparent tides in the lakes exhibit any characteristics of a similar connexion. That there is a frequent rise and fall in the level of the lake waters is beyond dispute. And it is as certain, that these fluctuations, in some places, appear to be as independent of atmospheric, as of lunar, control. But while we are unable to refer them to one cause, it does not follow that they must be assigned to the other. Governor Cass did not annex to his observations any note of the "moon's southings" at the time. If there were the remotest probability that such a reference could be useful, it might still be done. But the utter discrepancy between all lunations, and the ebbs and floods noted down in his table, renders such a task supererogatory. If the table be examined throughout, there will probably not be found an instance where the time of high water tallies with the moon's southing, admitting the usual retardation. Even if there were several such instances, they ought to be regarded as fortuitous coincidences, as nothing but a prevailing concurrence would authorize us to link them together as cause and effect.

It may be well to draw a few facts from the table, to show the irregularity and caprice of the times of high water. To avoid any appearance of making partial selections, we begin at the first dates. July 15th, it was high water at half past 7, P. M. the 16th, at half past 8, P. M. the 17th, at 8, A. M. the 18th, at noon, and again at half past 7, P. M. the 19th, at 9, A. M. the 20th, at 4, P. M. the 21st, at half past 7, P. M. the 22d, at 4, P. M. the 23d, at 4, P. M. the 24th, at 4, P. M. the 25th, at half past 7, P. M. Making allowance for a part of the night, during which no observations were made, the intervals would still appear without the slightest accordance with planetary attraction. They rather, so far as these instances go, evince something like a diurnal variation, arising from some local atmospheric habitude. Upon reference, however, to the course of the wind, as stated to have prevailed during those days, we do not find any such alternations of its currents, as would sustain such an opinion.

It will be seen, as we have before remarked, that the changes of elevation are independent of the course of the winds; that the fluctuations continue, notwithstanding the winds remain the same. Governor Cass suggests a reason why the Fox river should fall, even while the wind blows strongly up the bay and into its mouth. If a northerly wind prevail for some days, as it often does, down Lake Michigan, although it would, for a time, heap up the waters at the head of Green Bay (which runs nearly parallel with the lake,) while propelling a still greater mass towards the head of the lake, yet, the consequent depression of the level at the mouth of the bay, would soon cause a refluence of the accumulation at its head, even against the strength of the wind. This accounts for the contrariety of wind and current during a long storm; but it does not appear to apply to the diurnal, and even hourly, ebbs and floods which almost constantly succeed each other, whether the wind be blowing or not. A conjecture of some plausibility is suggested by inspecting the general course of the winds, as they are noted down in the table. Their prevailing course is up or down the bay, whose direction is about S. S. W. This would naturally have a tendency to roll the surface of the waters into waves, not very unlike those of the lunar tide, excepting their more frequent succession. These waves, whether refluent, or moving before the wind, in passing through the sinuous channel of the embouchure of Fox river, would be compressed into an increased elevation, and may be supposed to exhibit such intervals of fluctuation, as have been so long noticed at that place.

In speculating on the supposed tides of the North American Lakes, it has been natural to regard the head of Green Bay as the point where they would show themselves in the greatest fullness. The course of planetary attraction, operating on a line from east to west, would begin at the eastern part of Gloucester bay in Lake Huron, and moving over this lake to the Straits of Mackina, and thence across the foot of Lake Michigan and up Green Bay, would traverse a space of from four hundred and fifty to five hundred miles. The configuration of the coasts too, through which the line passes, would appear to lend much extraneous aid, to give whatever wave might be formed an undue elevation; as, after crossing Lake Huron, it would be compressed into the tunnel, or rather triangular form of that part of the lake which terminates at Mackina, causing a convolution, which would naturally send it through the straits into lake Michigan with added height and impetuosity. Again, when the wave, after traversing the foot of Lake Michigan, still somewhat preserved in its artificial elevation, by a chain of islands that run almost the whole breadth of this transit, enters Green Bay, the same tendency to accumulation must prevail throughout the ascent of that deep arm of the lake. The extent of Lake Superior is not equal in length to the course here described, and that lake, excepting the projection of Keweena Point, presents but few littoral features which would have any sensible influence on the elevation of a tide-wave.

But it must be borne in mind, in reference to this subject, that the planetary attraction, on reaching the eastern point of these lakes, having brought with it no "wave," has there to begin with an initial force, and that it must pass over a considerable portion of the water before its operation can be felt. We cannot say at what distance from the eastern shore this point of sensible effect would be found; but, if Lake Huron were an isolated lake, we should probably look for no lift of the surface, from this cause, even at the western side. The tide-wave, therefore, when it arrives at the Straits of Mackina, is, notwithstanding the favoring approximation of the two shores, probably nearly or quite insensible. It is well known that, although currents and counter currents have been long noticed in these straits, no one has ever regarded them as possessing any of the characteristics of a lunar tide. Even the fact stated by Charlevoix, and to which Mr. Schoolcraft alludes in his travels, of his boat floating one way while the wind blew the reverse, may be satisfactorily explained. A continuous and strong wind prevailing either way through the straits, will propel so much water out of one lake into the other, as to destroy the equilibration of surface; when the refluent tendency of the accumulated mass will produce a counter current, though the wind may remain unchanged and unabated. Hence Charlevoix's boat may have been "carried against a head wind."

If then it be probable that there is no sensible tide at the Straits of Mackina, Lake Michigan, including Green Bay, must be considered as deriving little or no assistance, in forming its tide-wave, from the sister lake. That it would exhibit this phenomenon, if it stood alone, few would be inclined to believe, notwithstanding all auxiliary circumstances, of the chain of islands, and the tunnel form of the bay. Indeed, Lake Michigan, though favorable for the increase of a wave sent into it from lake Huron, yet, from its comparative shallowness and diminutive breadth, seems unfavorable to the formation of one on its own bosom.

It is not to be assumed that planetary influences are wholly inoperative on the lake waters. They undoubtedly have their due effect. But that effect is probably nearly or quite insensible. If a calm could be supposed to prevail on the lakes of a sufficient continuance to allow these influences to act without disturbance from other causes, nice observations, at different points, would doubtless detect a small lunar tide. But such a halcyon lapse of time is improbable, if not impossible. And as long as shifting winds, or even breezes, are continually varying the surface of the waters, they will so interfere with these delicate tumefactions caused by the moon, as wholly to disguise or overpower them.

Reasoning from our knowledge of the great inland waters of the other hemisphere, we should take it for granted, that the North American Lakes have no sensible tide. The Caspian, Black and Baltic seas are said to have none; and even the Mediterranean is indebted to the sharpsightedness of modern times, for the developement of such a phenomenon on her wide spread bosom.

As General Dearborn has thrown out a hint respecting the supposed tide in Lake Superior, I have obtained a communication from H. R. Schoolcraft, Esq. on that subject. His long residence at the foot of that lake, combined with his enlightened powers of observation, and habitual use of them in the furtherance of scientific objects, give much weight to his opinions. Governor Cass, whose opportunities have been great, not only to see himself, but to collect the opinions of others, is satisfied that there is no sensible lunar tides on the lakes.

"DETROIT, January 19th, 1831.

MAJ. HENRY WHITING.—*Dear Sir*,—The idea of the existence of a tide in our lakes, caused by lunar attraction, appears to have originated in those changes in the level of the waters, which are produced by atmospheric phenomena. These changes were observed at a very early day, and they have continued to be observed, by travellers and by the resident population, down to our own times. The attention you formerly bestowed upon the subject, induces me to hope that you will resume your observations, and give the result of them to the public, in such a form as may enable others to judge of these phenomena, and the particulars wherein they differ—if, as I believe, they do indeed differ, from the ordinary, and from any known appearances of oceanic tide. I know not that your own observations will go the length of these conclusions, or that the conclusions themselves are based on remarks, which can be fully brought to mind. But I will endeavor to put you in possession of some facts bearing on the subject.

During a residence of nine years on the straits of St. Mary, near the foot of Lake Superior, I have remarked that the waters of those straits, and of Lake Superior, are particularly exposed to the influence of winds, which, for the greater portion of time, prevail either up or down the lake and the straits, thus subjecting them to an influence in the direction in which they are susceptible of being most affected by currents of wind. The effects are, a swelling in the waters at the point opposite to that at which the force is put in motion; and a recession of the waters whenever this force is abstracted. The rise and fall thus produced, have much of the appearance of a tide. The waters often overflow the banks; and they may recede, and again overflow the same portions of shore, twice, or oftener, during the same day.

Owing to counter currents of air, either in the higher or lower strata of the atmosphere, or to positive changes in the current of the wind itself, the results are varied, and the periods of submersion and recession rendered longer or shorter. Sometimes the water will re-act against the wind; sometimes it will continue to rise, when the wind itself has apparently (that is at the spot of observation) died away. Sometimes there will be little rise or fall, during the twenty four hours. And it is only during a calm, and that continued long enough, and in itself perfect enough, to leave the waters subject only to the operation of these ordinary laws, that an apparently level and equable surface is preserved in the lake.

But it is these variations in the *time*, the *height* of water and the *number* of the changes in any *given time*, that (without any reference to atmospheric phenomena) afford, to my mind, the most conclusive evidence that the changes in the diurnal or periodical level of the water, are separate and distinct, in their causes, from lunar tides.

The appearances of a tide rising against the wind, noticed by Captain Dearborn at the head of the military mill-race at the Sault St. Marie, admit of explanation on the principle of a reaction of the body of water, confined in that portion of the strait (about ten miles) situated between the head of the race (which is also the head of the falls) and lake Superior.

Very respectfully, your obedient servant,

HENRY R. SCHOOLCRAFT."

Before these desultory remarks are closed, it may not be inappropriate to notice what General Dearborn terms "the periodical increase and diminution of the whole volume of water on the lakes." It is the popular tradition on these lakes, that there has been a rise and fall of water once in every fourteen years. The New York canal commissioners, I believe, state it to be about once in eleven years. It is now a matter of record, that in 1814 and 15, the St. Clair and Detroit rivers were unusually high; that the foundations of houses, and much land that had long been under dry cultivation, were submerged. These buildings had been erected many years before, and of course under a belief that they were aloof from all but extraordinary and temporary inundations. No observations appear to have been made on the progress of the elevation, whether it were gradual or abrupt, or whether there were any preceding seasons of a character to produce it. The general impression seemed to be that the rise had been gradual, in accordance with the popular notion, that the waters rise seven years, and subside through the same period.

In 1820, or about that time, the rivers had resumed their usual level. Several wharves were built at Detroit between that year and 1828, at a height, as it was supposed sufficiently above the general level, for all purposes of convenience and safety. At the latter date, the rivers had again attained the elevation of 1815, and remained so until 1830, with only such occasional depressions as might be caused by strong winds, being generally nearly upon a level with the wharves. In this instance, like that of the foregoing, no observations appear to have been made previous to the rise, either on the character of the seasons, or the rapidity with which it reached its maximum.

The rivers continued at this unusual height until January, 1831, when, in the course of eight or ten days, they subsided three or four feet; and they have now maintained that minimum level for about six weeks. Two hydraulic works which had been established in connexion with the river the last season, were left by this subsidence, above high water mark, and their source-pipes have been extended many yards towards the channel, in order to reach a new supply.

In conversations with several of the old inhabitants of Detroit and its vicinity, it has been ascertained that there was a corresponding rise in the water about 1800. A road, running along the bank of the river near the town, was then nearly submerged, as it has been twice since.

Such are the simple facts and traditions relative to this phenomenon of the lakes. Being on this station in 1815, I witnessed the elevation at that time, and the subsequent depression. I was again there just before the rise in 1828, and have marked the continued elevation since that time, until the recent subsidence. There is not the same certainty as it respects the elevation of 1800; but there is no reason to doubt the concurring testimony of two or three respectable affirmers to the fact. The condition of the road—a great thorough-fare—alluded to, is a familiar and striking criterion, and likely to make an impression. There is no tradition, that we know, reaching farther back, excepting what may be inferred from the general belief of the old settlers, that the rise and fall is periodical as before stated.

As far as these facts go, they certainly favor the popular theory, but it rests on these facts alone. In every other point of view, it is improbable and seemingly absurd. There does not appear to have been any observations made on the character of the seasons immediately preceding and accompanying the elevation of the waters. We are therefore in the dark as to such causes as copious rains and abundant snows.

Abrupt and very considerable changes in the level of the Detroit river are frequently observed. Within twelve hours there will sometimes be a difference of two or three feet. But this may be satisfactorily accounted for. The Detroit river forms something like the arc of a circle, the two ends resting on Lake St. Clair and Lake Erie, whose courses continue the curve. A strong west or south-west wind drives back the waters of Lake St. Clair, thus diminishing the usual supply discharged into the river, and drives forward the waters of Lake Erie, thus lessening the volume and accelerating the current at the mouth of the river.

On the contrary, an easterly wind, driving down from Lake St. Clair an increased volume of water, and heaping it up equally at the outlet in lake Erie, causes an unusual elevation.

The sudden depression of the waters this winter, (1830–31,) before alluded to, is fresh in the recollection of every one, and if any obvious causes had preceded it, many would doubtless have observed them. It was observed that a strong westerly wind prevailed not long before. This would account for a temporary depression, upon the principles already explained, but for a temporary one only, as, even if Lake Erie were depressed many feet below its usual level, it is evident that the Detroit river would maintain its habitual height, provided the supply above continued the same; and in the present instance, that supply would of course return, the moment the westerly wind subsided, or the refluent tendency of the accumulated waters of the lake should overcome the resistance of that wind.

Mr. Schoolcraft has incidentally remarked, that it would appear natural for all the lakes to subside in a degree during the winter months. Evaporation and other wastes go on as during the summer months, though with diminished effects, while the ice and snow withhold from the tributary streams all the moisture of the earth's surface, and leave their channels almost dry. This opinion, so well founded in natural causes, is partly sustained by facts. It has been often observed that the ice, connected with the shore, is generally, before it breaks up or dissolves, found depressed below its first level. But this effect was not so sensible in the winters of 1828–9 and 1829–30, as to be noticed at Detroit.

From the foregoing remarks, the conclusion may be drawn, that there has been a periodical elevation of the upper lakes once in about fourteen years; or, that its recurrence has been sufficiently precise, to authorise the popular belief of its regularity. But we are constrained to suppose, although destitute of the light of all observations on the subject, that they must have been caused by unusually abundant rains and snows, and that this abundance has been in fortuitous coincidence with certain cycles of time; for, improbable as this may be, it is less so, than that nature should have departed from her ordinary course.

Since closing the foregoing remarks, I have been favored with the following letter from Gov. Cass, which expresses his opinion fully on the subject, and forms a valuable commentary on it.

"Detroit, March 24th, 1831.

Sir—In the conversation we had respecting the existence of tides in the lakes of this region, I referred to a series of observations, made by myself at Green Bay, in August and September, 1828, with a view to determine this long disputed question. This paper I now enclose to you, to dispose of as you think proper.* The place of observation was upon the Fox river, about three miles above its mouth, and two miles below the point, where the current ceases to be perceptible. A cask was securely placed near the bank, and a graduated rod fixed in it. The cask was sufficiently open to show the rise and fall of the water, without being affected by the ripples on the surface, occasioned by the wind. It was my intention to record the state of the water at regular intervals, and this, as you will perceive, was generally done. But sometimes circumstances intervened to withdraw my own attention, or that of others from this duty, to whom the task of observation was entrusted. Full confidence may however be placed in these memoranda.

---
*See the Table, page 194.

The slightest inspection will satisfy you, that the changes in the elevation of the water are entirely too variable to be traced to any regular permanent cause; and that consequently there is no perceptible tide at Green Bay, which is the result of observation. And such it appears to me is the result of calculation, when the laws, which regulate solar and lunar attraction, and the limited sphere of their operation, are taken into view. And the conclusion is fortified by analogy; for in the Baltic, the Black Sea, and the Caspian, each much larger than either of our lakes, there are no tides, or none worthy of observation. The opinion however has long prevailed, and been frequently advanced, that the ebb and flow of the water, which are constantly observed upon the shores of the North American lakes, are tides, governed by the same laws as the tides of the ocean: and Green Bay has been often referred to as a place affording the most distinct proof of this phenomenon; and particularly as the rise and fall of the water do not always appear to depend upon the direction of the wind. A glance at the features of the bay and lake, and at their relative position, will probably enable us to account for this prevailing error, without calling in question the veracity or judgment of preceding observers, or resorting to causes for the explanation of the difficulty, which have obviously no connexion with it.

Lake Michigan is about three hundred miles in length, and about fifty in breadth. Near its northern extremity, it is joined by Green Bay, which is in fact a deep indentation of the lake, nearly parallel with it in its course, and extending perhaps eighty miles into the country. A northerly wind blows up the bay and lake; and as the former is comparatively small, it will much sooner feel the full effect of the wind than the latter. The water will be driven from the mouth of the bay towards the head, until it attains its maximum elevation; and in the mean time, the operation of the same cause will propel the water of Lake Michigan towards Chicago. There will consequently be a depression at the mouth of the bay, where the water will continue to ebb, after it has risen to its full height in the upper part of the bay. For the wind, it will be recollected, is still sweeping up Lake Michigan, and driving the water before it. It is obvious that in this state of things a reaction must take place in Green Bay, and that the water will begin to flow towards the mouth, to supply the deficiency, occasioned by the transfer of a part of the contents of Lake Michigan, from the northern to the southern extremity; and this too, while the duration and intensity of the wind remain the same. At the head of the bay, the phenomenon will thus be exhibited, of the recession of the water in the face of a strong current of wind. This occurrence has no doubt led to the opinion already referred to, and the same appearances will be exhibited, though in a less striking degree, upon the shores of all the lakes. A slight variation in the force, or direction of the wind, will occasion a change in the elevation of the water, seeking at all times to attain a level; and alternations of ebbing and flowing will thus be exhibited, aided no doubt by the conformation of the coast, not easily reconcilable to the actual state of the wind.

Very respectfully, your obedient servant,

L. CASS.

Maj. Henry Whiting, U. S. A.

NOTE.

Since the preceding observations were sent to Silliman's Journal, cursory memoranda have been kept of the variations in the level of the Detroit river, which are herewith appended, as farther data to guide opinions respecting the supposed periodical character of these variations. They were not kept with much precision, as the main object was merely to ascertain that character. All observers are aware that the river is very sensibly affected by winds that strongly prevail in any one direction. No proofs are needed to confirm this fact. But preceding observations seeming to sustain the popular theory of a septennial rise and fall on the lakes, it was important to determine the truth or probability of it by more particular notices than have heretofore been recorded. The inference from such remarks as were warranted at the time the preceding article was written, and the notes which follow, will be, that, however regular the rise and fall has been heretofore, or previously to 1828, no subsidence, for any length of time, has taken place since. The level of the river, since that time, has been, through the season of navigation, pretty generally at the maximum height. At the minimum height, such as prevailed in 1817-18, and probably, in 1808-09, most of the vessels, of any burden, which passed from Lake Erie to Lake Huron, were obliged to unlade, in part, on the flats at the head of Lake St. Clair. Since 1828, such a necessity has never once existed, when vessels took the right channel.

The guage by which the following results have been obtained is a simple one, and not fitted to give them with much nicety. But nicety, though desirable, was not essential. The object in view was fully attained, by taking the wharf built by Mr Oliver Newberry, and now owned by the public, and marking the changes which were exhibited by its sides. The timbers are about a foot square. By casting upon them a most cursory glance, the difference in the level of the waters would at once be perceived, within a very few inches.

During the summer of 1830, the river was generally nearly on a level with the bottom of the upper timber, or about one foot down. It was unusually high that season—higher than it has been at any subsequent season.

January, 1831. About the middle of this month, the ice, which was nearly upon a level with the top of the wharf, sunk four feet in the course of a few days, and remained at that minimum about six weeks, when the river began gradually to rise again. The ice during that period was frequently broken up and dispersed. The prevailing winds had been strongly in the S. W.

April 19, 1831.		Within one foot of the top of the wharf.
21,	"	Six inches do. wind easterly and strong.
May 4,	"	Two feet do. 11 oclock A. M. wind westerly and strong. 4 o'clock P. M. 2 1-2 feet, wind do.
" 5,	"	8 o'clock A. M. 1 1-2 feet.
" 9,	"	9 o'clock A. M. 1 1-2 feet, wind N. W. gentle. 2 " P. M. 2 feet, do. strong.
" 11,	"	10 " A M. 2 feet, do. W. strong.
June 16,	"	Generally at about 1 foot, generally calm.
Sept. 7,	"	Little variaton in the level since last memorandum. Summer rather wet.
Oct 26,	"	Same remarks. Sept. very wet
Nov. 19,	"	2 1-2 feet. Wind. for two days, strongly S. S.W.
" 22,	"	2 3-4 feet. Wind moderate do
Dec. 10,	"	River closed with ice. Water on the top of it, upon a level with the wharf, winds not high.
Dec. 20,	"	Ice sunk about three feet.
" 26,	"	do. about four feet. River continues to be frozen over, having been only partially broken up since the 10th ultimo.
Feb. 9, 1832.		Ice gone. River 2 1-2 feet. Much snow during the month of January.
" 20,	"	River one foot from the top of the wharf, having been gradually rising since last memorandum, much snow, and some rain during the month.
" 24,	"	Ther. 8 o'clock A. M. 10 degrees below zero (Third time this winter.) River closed in one night Ice upon a level with the wharf.
Mar 20,	"	River two feet.
April 1,	"	River 1 1-2 " month of March dry.
" 5,	"	River 1 foot.
" 15,	"	River 1 1-2 feet, month thus far dry.
Nov. 20,	"	" 2 1-2 " summer rather dry.
Dec. 8,	"	" 2 3-4 "
" 11,	"	" 2 1-2 " much rain.
Mar. 2 1833.		River closed for the first time this season. Ther. 8 o'clock A. M, three deg. below zero Five deg. above, at the same hour, the lowest before during the winter. Month of December, mild and wet; January cool enough to keep the surface of the earth frozen, and make good roads, but pleasant, and neither snow nor rain. February snowy, good sleighing throughout. Level of the River, at an average, 3 1-2 feet.
Mar. 18,	"	Level of the River the same.
" 25,	"	River 3 feet. Ice gone, and water rising. Severe thunder storm 20th.
" 30,	"	River 3 feet. No rain during the month, excepting the thunder storm
May 4,	"	River 3 feet, having varied little since the last memorandum Spring dry.
July 8,	"	River 2 feet, for a few weeks past, much rain in the mean time.
Sept. 10,	"	River 2 1-2 feet, occasionally a little lower Summer very dry.
Oct. 8,	"	River 2 3-4 feet. Subsiding since the last memorandum, though considerable rain has fallen.

Oct. 19, "   River 3 feet, much rain, but strong westerly winds. A most tempestuous season. More wrecks on the lake than have occurred for past several years.
Nov. 15, "   River 3 feet. Wet season, but westerly winds.
Jan. 20, 1834. Ice on a level with the top of the wharf. Much snow, preceded by abundant rains.
" 31, "   River 3 1-2 feet. River closed most of the time since the last memorandum.
Febr. 5, "   River 4 feet. No ice. Weather dry.
" 10, "   "   3 1-2 "   Little snow or rain.
Mar. 10, "   "   3   "   No ice. Weather generally fair.
" 28, "   "   2 3-4 "   Wet weather.
May 1. "   "   2 1-2 "   Same throughout the month. Dry month.
July 16, "   River 2   "   Much rain.
Aug. 1, "   "   1 1-2 "

CPSIA information can be obtained
at www.ICGtesting.com
Printed in the USA
LVHW111945230122
709154LV00008B/914